THE LAW OF

ACTION

Gain Perfect Clarity, Boost Your Confidence and Get More Results *NOW*

THE LAW OF
ACTION

Gain Perfect Clarity, Boost Your
Confidence and Get More Results
NOW

ROB ACTIS

Paperback ISBN: 978-1-948839-01-3
Digital ISBN: 978-1-948839-00-6

Cover Design: *Kristen Sibayan*
Editing: *Tammi Metzler, WriteAssociate.com*
Content Editing: *Andrea Nicole King*
Interior Design: *Christina Gorchos, 3CsBooks.com*
Cover and Interior Photo: *Patricia Sweeny*

DEDICATION

This book is dedicated to my amazing daughter Aidan. You continue to inspire me in all the challenges you overcome. You move through any obstacle in your path. Your warrior spirit, fearlessness, and determination are truly inspiring. I feel humbled and blessed to be your father.

And to Tanya. I had no idea the day I met you that you would become such an integral part of my life. You're always there for me, cheering me on. Everything about you is beautiful. You continue to inspire me to greatness. Life with you is beyond fun.

We interrupt this book to bring you a special, last-minute update...

My book is about 98% done, and I'm having doubts.

I added this message right here in the beginning because this is what I need to tell you before you even start chapter one. I write this to you because in this book, I am committed to being authentic and sharing my vulnerabilities. We all have self-doubts. We all have those reels that run in our head of "I'm not good enough" or "I'm not worthy". We sometimes feel afraid of failure, or even success.

We worry... What if it doesn't work?

They hit me like a ton of bricks today. All these voices that I've heard growing up from my stepdads and other people in my life who said, "You're dumb. You're not worthy. Why don't you get a real job? You can't do that." They all came and enveloped me like a raging tornado of emotion. It stopped me dead in my tracks. I thought to myself, "Why would anybody want to hear what I have to say? Why would anyone want to hear my story? Who am I to say others should take action?"

It paralyzed me, to a point where I actually wanted to just stop writing the book. I felt like a fraud. It was devastating.

The thing is, I've always taken action in my life. Whenever I've met adversity, I still pushed through and have had great success. However, the imposter syndrome, fear of failure, and "I'm not worthy" anxiety, all which I talk about in this book, came up for me to deal with just now. So I sat down and meditated about why I am writing this book.

Before I could finish it, I had to check in. I asked myself if I was in alignment with my life's purpose. I questioned what my motivation was for doing this book. What came up was that my motivation is to help people get out of the planning phase and move into action to have their hopes and dreams realized. Right? Is that really it? I had to do a gut check.

"Yes," came the answer.

Once I got that embodied in my core, I was able to get back to the 2% of writing left to finish this book.

I am the action guy. I am 100% committed to not only living the Law of Action but also to teaching the Law of Action to as many people as are willing to experience it and break through limiting fears.

I am the right person, and I have accomplished a lot in my life. I have overcome many, many obstacles. I sat in a hospital room next to my daughter, telling her, "Please don't die. I need you. The world needs you.

I've had a doctor look me in the eyes and say, "If you would have come to this hospital about an hour from now, you would have been dead."

I am here today to get my story out because I am 100%—no, 1000%—committed to inspiring others and being a catalyst for transformation. I know 1000% doesn't really exist but the reason I say that is because I am ALL IN.

I almost stopped this book at the very end because of fear. I almost let self-doubt stop me from taking the action needed to achieve my dreams. Many others do the same, but this book is meant to get you past that fear and into inspired, life-changing action.

I am humbled and honored that you are reading the Law of Action. I hope you find it a catalyst in your journey forward.

A SPECIAL INVITATION

THE LAW OF ACTION IS A POWERFUL WAY to gain perfect clarity, boost your confidence and get more results now!

If you're looking for a community to connect with virtually, just visit www.thelawofaction.com/community.

You'll be able to connect in my Facebook Group with other motivated action takers and be part of a movement which can inspire millions.

I'll be popping in often to read about your amazing successes, so please do share them. Watch for opportunities to interact live with me, and also find links to resources to support you as you Decide, Plan, and Act.

Connect with Rob:

Actis Publishing LLC
929 N Val Vista Drive
Suite 109-102
Gilbert, AZ 85234

480-9000-ROB
support@thelawofaction.com
Facebook: www.facebook.com/RobActisAuthor
Twitter: @freshvo
Instagram: @robactis

CONTENTS

Foreword

By Hal Elrod

WHEN I MET ROB IN 2013, HE HAD auditioned to be the narrator for my book, *The Miracle Morning.* I didn't know then that *The Miracle Morning* would become a series, but here we are in 2018, and Rob has narrated all eight of *The Miracle Morning* books, with many more to come. He told me that when he began narrating the first one, as he read it, he began to put the Miracle Morning process into practice. He said it changed his life.

Over the years, Rob has continued to be not only the voice of *The Miracle Morning* series, but also a supportive friend and associate.

When Rob told me he was writing a book and asked me to write a Foreword for it, I felt it reinforced the importance of working together and inspiring each other to greatness. This is why we are here—to help each other. We each have a unique piece of the puzzle to contribute which can inspire people to take action and ownership in their life. I'm all for that.

The Miracle Morning provides a framework to create in. Interestingly, the Law of Action fits perfectly with it to offer a repeatable process. Puzzle pieces. With so many ways to climb the mountain, and so many tools to get there, I feel the Law of Action will appeal to people who are ready to take the next steps to achieve greatness but don't know where to start.

Not only does the book provide simple, tangible ways to do things like increasing productivity or meeting a new person, it also includes inspiring stories. Rob shares his own accounts of challenges he has faced and overcome. He also has included stories and interviews about people in his life. People who have gotten stuck. People who have failed. These are real and vulnerable stories which help bring the Law of Action into an understandable practice. They are about people who are now successful but haven't always been.

Whether you already consider yourself to be highly successful—or if becoming successful is something you're committed to—this is the book that can significantly accelerate your success.

Hal Elrod
Author of the #1 bestselling book,
*The Miracle Morning: The Not-So-Obvious Secret
Guaranteed to Transform Your Life*

Foreword

By Mike Koenigs

ROB ACTIS LIVES AND BREATHES THE "LAW OF ACTION." He's easily one of if not the most coachable people I've ever met who's willing to listen, learn, implement and examine his behaviors, mindset and habits to be effective. And that's why you want to read this book. Rob invests a tremendous amount of time and money into gaining clarity, boosting confidence and getting results.

Let me put this in perspective for you. I've had the great fortune of having over 54,000 clients and customers in 121 different countries as of right now. I've coached and consulted millionaires, billionaires, celebrities and bestselling authors including Tony Robbins, Paula Abdul, Richard Dreyfuss, JJ Virgin, John Assaraf, Brian Tracy, Xprize founder Peter Diamandis, Jorge Cruise, Harvey Mackay, Daniel Amen and publisher of *Success* Magazine, Darren Hardy. I've helped create over 1,600 bestselling authors worldwide with my systems.

Rob has been a client for years. I have the great fortune of coaching him and supporting his dreams and the honest truth is, it's easy because he's done the deep work on himself that brings a constant stream of success and abundance in his life.

And that's why you want to read this book. Rob is interesting because he's *interested*. He's a great teacher because he's a great *student*. He's successful because he's humble. And when you accept him as your guide, he'll help you achieve the promise he makes in his book:

The Law of Action: Gain Perfect Clarity, Boost Your Confidence and Get More Results NOW.

My prediction is that Rob is going to continue his path to even greater success and abundance. He'll continue to grow his arsenal of tools and resources that make him even more effective. The question is, are you willing to let him bring you on a journey to discover your highest version of yourself?

The next step is easy. Just turn the page. And the next page. And the next. Listen, learn, implement. Let Rob be your guide.

Mike Koenigs
CEO and *Chief Disruptasaurus*, You Everywhere Now

A Note From Rob

GUESS WHAT?

You already took action by picking up this book. Congratulations!

Maybe you don't even need this book. Wait, who am I KIDDING? *Everyone* needs the Law of Action described in these pages. Thank you for taking the time to read this book that I've put my heart and soul into.

It's normal to get stopped by fear when we have big dreams in front of us. We sometimes don't feel worthy, and often fear takes over and blocks our progress.

Speaking of fear and unworthiness... When I decided to write *The Law of Action*, I thought to myself, "Am I really worthy of writing the book on the Law of Action?"

That question consumed my thoughts throughout the writing process; however, I know now that I am the right person to bring to you the Law of Action. In writing this book and revisiting the path of my life, I realize I have been using the Law of Action the whole time! I have used it to achieve extraordinary results and bring many dreams into reality.

Now, I am committed, not only to continue taking action in my life but also to support others in taking action in their lives. This book will show you how to conquer your fears so you can have the life of your dreams.

The Law of Action is Beyond the Law of Attraction

The movie and the book, *The Secret*, has spread the concepts of the Law of Attraction. I'm sure you loved it; I certainly did. Full disclosure: I'm into vision boards, I believe in affirmations, and I have seen the power of thinking positive thoughts, but I've always felt in my gut that something was missing.

Unfortunately, some people who have learned the Law of Attraction seem to think they can just sit on a couch, waiting for their lives to magically change. What they don't know is that if you don't take action, nothing happens.

Actually, let me elaborate on that, because if you don't take action, things *can* happen. But those are often things you don't *want* showing up in your life.

Do I know the consequences of not taking action? Yes, I do. I almost died from not taking action. Really, almost died, like one hour away from a slow and painful death. I'll tell you more about that later. Do I personally believe that taking action is one of the most important things you can do in your life?

Yes. 100%. Absolutely.

That's why I'm so excited to share this with you. I've had lots of life experiences and have learned by watching others' life experiences. Through that, I have identified the process I've been using all along to inspire and teach other people to not get stuck in the planning stage, but to instead get out there and take action.

Because when you take action, great things happen.

So, if you're ready, I'd like to introduce you to the Law of Action.

Strap in and hold on tight. Please keep your hands and arms inside the vehicle at all times. This is an E ticket ride. For all you millennials out there, you young'uns, an E ticket was from this incredible, magical, happiest place on Earth called Disneyland, and the best rides were E ticket rides. This was long before the FastPass+, way back in the day we had to actually use tickets to get on a ride and we only got a handful of E tickets. This is your E ticket ride, because your life will be forever transformed when you follow the Law of Action.

Inspiring you to take action,

INTRODUCTION

By Rob Actis

NOBODY GOES THROUGH LIFE WITHOUT CHALLENGES.

Most successful people have overcome incredible odds to get to where they are, and everybody's path is different. Some have it easier than others, and some handle the challenges more gracefully.

I welcome you to this book to not only share my experiences and stories but to also invite you to see the reality behind authentic human experiences of over a dozen highly successful entrepreneurs.

They've been there. They've done that. They got the shirt, not just a participation ribbon. Now they are sharing their stories with a vulnerability and openness that will inspire you to take the next steps toward your greatness.

You don't have to be an entrepreneur to use the Law of Action, though. It can apply to anyone, in any situation and any walk of life. When you use it completely and repeatedly, you can create anything you desire.

And the best part? The Law of Action consists of just three steps:

Decide. Plan. Act.

Those three things give you the simple process to follow so you can do something as straightforward as mindfully making a sandwich, or make your goal a little more complex, like planning to earn a million dollars.

It's all the same plan, the same three steps. The magic is in actually applying it.

In my life, I've experienced plenty of challenges to bring me to this moment, and I wouldn't change a thing.

Taking Action in the Face of Seemingly Impossible Obstacles

My first big challenge came when I was just five years old and my parents divorced.

I experienced a few stepdads as I grew up, and the idea that I wasn't worthy was hammered into my brain by those stepdads. Yet another challenge I had to overcome.

Luckily, I was a precocious little kid, and my desire to succeed was strong. When I was just four years old, I stood in front of my family as we watched "Laugh In" with Gary Owens.

After hearing the opening announcement, "Live from downtown Burbank," I turned around and declared to my family, "I want to talk on TV!"

At four, I really had no idea what that really meant, but apparently that's when some part of me declared that I wanted to talk on TV.

As early as age seven, I played "radio". I was fascinated by this game. I pretended I was the DJ on the radio, using an audio cassette recorder and my record players. (For you millennials, if you don't know what an audio cassette recorder or record player is, Google it. No, seriously...)

Little did I know that I was living the Law of Action! I had no idea that someday, when I was a 53-year-old man, I'd share this story with the world. All throughout my childhood, I was just following my heart and doing what I loved.

I wanted to be on the radio as a disc jockey. I listened to Casey Kasem religiously every weekend. I listened to all the radio stations. I love music, but the one thing that I listened to the most was the disc jockeys talking.

I remember listening to Shotgun Tom Kelly on KCBQ religiously and saying, "I want to do that."

In my later years, he became a peer, working at the same radio station. He gave me lots of great advice that helped me in my radio career.

Thank you, "Shotz".

This radio legend is now a good friend of mine (talk about *mind blown*), and I'm proud to say, he has earned a star on the Hollywood Walk of Fame.

But it took a while to actually work in radio; I kept taking steps to get to that point yet sadly, when I talked about that dream, especially as a little kid, people were not supportive of me because it's "not a real job." My progress was slow going, to say the least.

I wanted to be in radio, on TV, that person in front of the room. And for some amazing reason, I chose even as a kid to take action in those directions, even though most people thought I was dumb and that I should do something else.

Whenever I got the chance, I would ask to speak into the microphone, whether that was making announcements or finding other ways to get in front of groups of people. Heck, I even used to perform magic. Anything I could do to be in front of crowds, engaging people.

By sixth grade, I helped out with school assemblies. In seventh grade, I went to a school with grades seven through twelve and discovered that I could make announcements over the school PA system. All I had to do was ask.

I went right into the media center and asked one of the audio visual (AV) teachers, Linda Sotello, "Can I be the one to make the announcements?"

Her response was, "Well, students don't really do that," but then...I did that. Somebody had to tell everybody else about the pep rally at noon. It used to be teachers, but after I asked, that somebody became me.

I hung out in the library a lot because there was a media room. I had two AV teachers, Monte Ocoha and Linda Sotello, as I mentioned previously. Yep, same Linda. I will never forget her.

I didn't like to be at home much, so I stayed after school for hours and hours. Linda managed the AV room, and she would let me "play radio" where they had reel to reel players, audio cassette recorders, record players, and a microphone. Instead of telling me it was "dumb" or downplaying my goal, she let me go in there and hone my craft.

I actually played radio and made announcements all the way through ninth grade. Then we moved.

I had to start fresh, so I asked to start a radio station at my new school.

I did the announcements for that school too. I also started DJing at the school dances with my friend Ron. We had turntables and everything. It was great.

Getting Closer Every Day

When I followed my heart and did what I loved, it was amazing how things just showed up to support me.

As evidenced by a cool thing that happened when I was about sixteen. I worked at a grocery store, and one of the cashiers, Vicki, also worked at a local radio station. She was a weekend disc jockey, and she let me go to the radio station—KKOS, channel 96.5 in Carlsbad—with her. I would go up there on the weekends to play in the studio, do commercials and sit in the booth when she was on the air. It was incredible, a dream come true.

I was in heaven. She would coach me, because she saw my passion and interest in radio. It was amazing. I had always wanted to be a disc jockey, and here I was taking action and getting closer to that goal.

During high school, my favorite radio station was B100 FM. I listened all the time. One of my favorite DJ's was Danny Wilde, who did the afternoon drive. I used to call him on the request line every once in a while, and he was really kind to me. One day I just asked him if I could come up to the radio station and sit in the booth with him while he was on the air.

He said yes.

It was an unbelievable experience and a great example of how amazing things can happen if you just ask.

Going Back Home

Everything was good until things changed at home. My latest stepdad and I didn't get along at all. It was bad.

Thank God for my sister, Anita. She had a conversation with my mom, and I was able to escape my stepdad and move in with my sister.

I was back in my old neighborhood. Back home with my friends.

Without missing a beat, I enrolled in the TV production class. It was awesome; we had our own news show and produced other programs as well. I worked for the news channel as a reporter. By my senior year of high school, I had worked as an anchor and a reporter on Q-News, the closed-circuit news program that was circulated through my high school and which every student was forced to watch (my apologies to my fellow alumni!). I missed a lot of class and don't necessarily know if that was a good thing...but I was a pretty hyper kid and I think the teachers actually loved not having me in class! And it gave me some great opportunities to do things on and off campus.

One of my best achievements that I was able to shoot off campus was a senior project called "Everything You've Always Wanted to Know About the Prom but Were Afraid to Ask."

I wanted to go to the prom but it was really expensive, of course, so I had the idea to get paid advertising from local businesses so that they would pay for the prom instead of me.

I decided to approach local businesses that supplied things for prom.

The florist I asked was more than happy to give me some free flowers in exchange for mention in my video, which was going to be shown to all the seniors at my high school.

Of course, I needed a limo, so I went and got a deal with a limo company.

And then a tuxedo, so I made a deal for a tuxedo.

The Harbor House Restaurant in San Diego was cool enough to trade me advertising for dinner. (Wonderful place, by the way. It's still there as of this writing in 2018.)

Not only did I get my entire prom paid for, I also got an A plus on that assignment. I decided, and then I took action. I asked for what I wanted.

I realize now that I was starting to master the art of asking when I was pretty young. I'm so glad I did.

An Unbelievable Opportunity?

After high school, one of my friends told me that he was buying a radio station in Steamboat Springs, Colorado. He wanted me to work at the radio station.

I thought my life could never get any better.

Little did I know, this was not going to be my dream job. When I packed up and moved to Aurora, Colorado, they hadn't yet purchased the radio station.

He had me working in his real estate development company and oil and gas company.

Much to my dismay, they put me in an office, and I did accounting.

Accounting. Um, what?

I was in charge of filing and reconciling bank statements. That was a *nightmare*. While I waited for the radio station deal to happen, I became really bored. I didn't want to do the work I was doing, but there was this promise of (eventually) being in radio. I continued to wait it out until one day, I walked down the hallway of the office building and discovered a singing telegram company. I figured it would be another way to get in front of people, so I became a singing telegram person. In addition to that, I made friends at the local bar and helped them by doing the announcements for their promotions. Yes, I was only 18, but you could drink in a bar at 18 in Colorado. I had a lot of fun during those times.

That felt better. I remembered what I was supposed to be doing and got back on track.

It was time to take action. No more filing or bank reconciliation for this guy.

After a year of working in the office of the oil and gas company and real estate development company, bored out of my mind, I knew I needed to move home and get back to radio. So guess what I did? I quit. I packed up, got a U-Haul trailer, and drove fourteen hours to San Diego—during the blizzard of '83, mind you. I hate snow, just saying.

I got back to San Diego, and my mom let me live with her.

My *Real* Opportunity

My next step was to enroll in Grossmont College in La Mesa, California. There I met someone who opened the door for me to be in radio: my now long-time friend, Tony Pepper. He and I became fast friends, immediately hit it off.

Tony was on the radio at Grossmont College, so I would hang out with him in the station. I then enrolled in the radio class, and we started a morning show called the Rob and Tony morning show.

I was also working with Tony and another DJ at B100, Gary Kelley, as a mobile music DJ for weddings and corporate events.

It was during that stint that I met some guys at Minolta in San Diego when I was DJing for their holiday party. They liked me, and I liked them. I saw that they were making a boatload of money. I talked to this guy named Carmine, and he said, "Come on in for an interview." They wanted me to do telemarketing.

Well, let's just say that the first month, I was the third in sales in the entire country. I was making 125 calls a day, and my first paycheck was thousands and thousands of dollars. That was back in the early '90s, when I was 20-something years old.

Despite my talent for it, I discovered that telemarketing wasn't the path I wanted. I didn't want to be a copier salesperson. I really wasn't motivated by money; I'm still not motivated by money. I know you need money to survive, but that's never been my main focus.

Meanwhile, Tony was still at B100 FM in San Diego, working on the air and also as a production person.

———————————————

One day when I was talking to Tony, I said, "I wish I could be on the radio. You're so lucky, man. You're a DJ at the number one radio station in San Diego. I want to do that."

An incredibly good guy who never minced words, Tony just looked at me for a moment before saying, "So, let me ask you a question. You want to be on the radio, right?"

"Absolutely."

"Have you ever thought of maybe going and applying to get a job at an actual radio station instead of calling people all day trying to sell copiers?"

"No."

He goes, "What, did you just think that someone was just going to discover you and knock on your door and put you on the radio?"

I replied, "Yes, that was actually exactly what I thought."

Tony told me I should apply at B100, so I did. And I got hired.

Then, what did I do? I walked into my boss's office at Minolta.

I said, "John, thank you so much for this opportunity."

He said, "You're doing great, man. You're like the top in sales. You might be number one next month."

I shook my head no. "I want to let you know that I'm quitting. I'm pursuing my dream of radio. And I have to quit." He was really quiet. You could've heard a pin drop.

Confused, he asked, "Did you see how much money you made this month?"

I said, "I did. And this is not getting me any closer to my dream of being on the radio."

"So, you want to go work as a receptionist at a radio station."

"Yep."

"And how much are they going to pay you?"

"$4.10 an hour."

He said, "I can't let you go."

I shrugged, "You've got to let me go."

I worked another week, and I was gone. I knew I was back on track when making $4.10 an hour was fine because I loved the work I was doing. I mean, I was technically a switchboard operator, answering the phones and transferring calls, but I was working in an actual radio station!

It turned out to be a 10- or 15-hour per week job, which certainly didn't pay me much, but the universe had lined me up with Tony Pepper and Gary Kelley in the mobile music business. I was doing lots of wedding receptions and corporate events, so that worked out great. I was in heaven.

Influenced by the Best

As I progressed through my twenties, I was living my dream. I started on the phones and paid my dues in the business. I surrounded myself with the people I wanted to be most like. I made my way back to the promotions department, where I worked with two very powerful women, Sandi Bannister and Joan Hiser, and also J.R. Rogers. I learned the ins and outs of the science of radio station promotions. Not to mince words, it was a lot of grunt work before the event. That's where I acquired my absolute distaste for blowing up balloons. I never want to blow up another balloon in my life.

I do need to say a special thank you to J.R. Rogers. One day we were setting up for a promotion and we needed to set up this giant inflatable balloon with the B100 FM logo on it. We got up on the roof, which I was totally not digging, and it was a windy day. We were letting the blower inflate this balloon, and all of a sudden, a big gust of wind came and took the inflatable with it. I will say that I was a very loyal employee (maybe too loyal?), so when the balloon was blowing off of the rooftop, I went after it; not my brightest idea. I grabbed for the inflatable, in the process nearly going over the side of the two-story building. J.R grabbed me and held on tight, the only thing that stopped me from falling to my death two stories down. Thanks, J.R. I was blessed to have been mentored by some very talented people during my radio career. Bobby Rich is the one who gave me my big break into radio. He coached and mentored me, along with creating a launching pad that I have really taken advantage of.

I became a radio personality in large part because I was so fortunate to be mentored by and work with such amazing talent. I'd also like to acknowledge Tony Pepper, Mike Novak, Gary Kelley, Ellen K, Danny

Romero, and Frank Anthony, just to name a few. Across the hall in the newsroom were Marilyn Hyder, Ian Rose and Gail Stuart, among others.

My career in radio evolved into voice acting, commercials, and many other opportunities.

I was talking on TV, and radio too; I felt my four-year-old self smiling within me.

Fast forward to today...

I am a voice actor for many national TV commercials and narrator for a long list of best-selling audio books, including *The Miracle Morning* Book series, books by Honorée Corder, and my most recent audio book project, *The Law of Action* by...oh yeah, me!

I own a successful creative agency producing voiceovers and videos. I also emcee many large corporate events, motivating and inspiring through my speaking engagements. The most fulfilling work I do now is as a strategic advisor of the Law of Action, coaching top-tier, six- and seven-figure business professionals who are following their heart like I did and who are committed to investing in their future goals and dreams but feel stuck in planning and need strategic guidance into taking decisive action. What does your story look like? I've shared with you a brief roadmap of my life path. It may seem pretty positive, like I have had an easy, "happily ever after" life.

But remember, nobody goes through life without challenges, and things can change in a split second, as you will see in chapter one.

Chapter 1

YOUR DAUGHTER MAY DIE

"There are risks and costs to action. But they are far less than the long range risks of comfortable inaction."

-JOHN F. KENNEDY

THE WORDS THAT NO PARENT EVER WANTS TO HEAR.

"Your daughter may die."

Your life can change in an instant.

I'm not gonna lie, this chapter is painful. It hurts. I have tears in my eyes just writing this. But I put it here, as the first chapter to help illustrate the power and consequences of taking action as well as those of *not* taking action. Also to show that my life isn't some unrealistic fairy tale, full of sugar and spice and everything nice. We all have troubles, we all face obstacles; it's how we handle everything that comes at us that makes the real difference.

Now, back to Aidan.

To give you a little background about my daughter, she has always been one of those "perfect" kids that seem almost too good to be true.

When she walked into a room, everybody just flocked to her.

Aidan could sing. She could dance. She was not afraid to be up on stage; in fact, she was on stage with me a lot. She really was a perfect kid.

This story is told from my point of view, and also from the memory of Aidan's mom, Nikki. Thank you, Nikki, for contributing to this. The journey we had with this experience leaves me forever grateful for your strength and ability to take massive action.

ROB:

June 8, 2013, seemed to be a normal day for our daughter, Aidan Actis.

NIKKI:

We planned a day of fun in the sun and mud! We were headed to the city of Scottsdale's Mud Mania, an annual day of mud obstacle courses, mud pits and fun getting dirty. Rob; Aidan; her boyfriend, Christian; and I were in for an exciting, fun day.

We spent all morning watching folks get dirty, laughing and enjoying Aidan and Christian competing against each other in the mud courses. All was great!

By about 1 p.m., we were all starving, so we got cleaned up as best as we could with fire hoses at the event and went to lunch. Mexican was the choice of the day.

We were worried they wouldn't let us into the restaurant since we were still pretty muddy, but it all worked out. Lunch was great. We talked about the fun we'd had earlier, and Aidan was giving Christian a hard time about beating him in the race. There were laughs all around.

We took Christian home and arrived back at our house about 4 p.m.

I urged Aidan to get in the shower and scrub the caked-in mud out of her hair.

ROB:

I was informed by Nikki that Aidan had a headache, so I went to check on her. She was upstairs in the guestroom, drawing a mermaid. (It was really good...Aidan is an amazing artist.)

So she had this terrible headache, and Nikki said she was probably very dehydrated. She reminded her of the active day we'd had, and how living in the desert, we need to drink lots of water, especially when doing strenuous activities outside. We gave her some ibuprofen and water and put her to bed. It had been a long day, and it seemed like if she got some rest she would be fine.

AIDAN:

It started like a headache, just normal. Then it got worse and then worse and then worse, to the point where I was crying. And then I was just ... I was done and I wanted to go to bed. I got sick and threw up, and then my parents came and checked on me. I couldn't speak, and my eyes got really wide. I was thinking, *What? Why can't I speak? What's wrong with me?*

NIKKI:

After lying down in her bed for about 20 minutes, Aidan had come to me still complaining of a horrible headache. I told her,

"See, you are dehydrated. Headaches are a sign of dehydration."

Rob was on the way to Five Guys to grab a few burgers, per Aidan's request. She really started complaining about her head hurting. I, honestly, was annoyed by it, thinking, *Come on kid, it's just a headache, chill.*

ROB:

As I was leaving, Aidan came out of her room and started throwing up in the bathroom. I mean, like, really throwing up. I didn't think too much of it, and teased her a bit, "What's the matter, Aidan? Did you have too much Mexican food?"

Figuring she'd be okay, I said, "All right. I love you guys," and walked out the door. I drove away, but then I had this weird feeling that something wasn't right; it was like nothing I'd ever felt before.

NIKKI:

Aidan was in the bathroom still throwing up. All I said was, "You're dehydrated," but I started feeling bad about giving her such a hard time about it. I got her a cool cloth to put on the back of her neck. As I walked into the bathroom, I asked her how she was feeling.

No response.

I asked again how she was feeling, and again no response. I was pissed.

I said, "Aidan, how are you feeling?" She then looked up at me and immediately our world changed.

ROB:

That was when Nikki called me. She was screaming.

"It's Aidan! It's Aidan! Rob, come home! Something's wrong... Aidan can't talk!"

I made an immediate U-turn. I drove incredibly fast, almost running over my neighbor who was crossing the street.

NIKKI:

I put my hand on Aidan's arm and asked her to talk to me. She looked confused, terrified. She was unable to get out a coherent sentence.

When Aidan finally looked up at me, the right side of her face had fallen; it was drooping. She was unable to answer me because she was having a stroke. My beautiful, sassy, smart 14-year-old daughter was having a stroke.

I assured her that all was okay, that Mommy and Daddy would get her to the hospital right away.

ROB:

I ran in the house and up the stairs. In a panic, I looked at my daughter and her mom, and I said, "What's going on? What's wrong? What's the matter? You can't talk?"

Her response was garbled, muffled ... and her mouth was droopy. I was so confused! How can a kid have a stroke?

NIKKI:

We lived about three miles from the hospital, thank God! We were able to get there very quickly.

Aidan was sitting in the front seat and I was talking to her from the back, my hands on her shoulders, reassuring her that we were almost there and that she was going to be okay. We were getting her help.

She seemed to slump lower and lower into the chair as we drove. What was happening? What the hell was going on?

We arrived at the hospital and rushed her in. We did not have a great reception from the ER staff! We told them what had happened and pleaded for someone to help.

ROB:

Aidan was not doing very well. I demanded that she be seen, and they told me to wait. I demanded again that she be seen loudly enough that we finally got in. They looked at her, then us, and said, "Is she pregnant? Is she on drugs? Has she been drinking?"

"NO! She had a stroke!"

They actually argued with me.

"No. She's a young child. She's a teenager. She must be pregnant or on drugs or ... "

I continued to get louder until we were taken back to a room, but they still weren't acting like it was an emergency. They were kind of slow to respond. We were panicking. I demanded attention and support for my daughter and didn't let up.

Another nurse came in and then all of a sudden, Aidan went away. She started to become unresponsive. That apparently got their attention, because the room was suddenly filled with 15 new people!

At that point, a woman walked up to Nikki and me and said, "You need to step away. We will handle it from here."

My response was to put my arm around Nikki and say, "We are not going anywhere." The woman put her hand on my shoulder, looked at us with a seriousness that gave me chills, and said, "This is really, really bad. You need to prepare for the worst. She may die."

You don't expect to hear that about your only child, your amazing daughter, whom you just had a great, fun day with.

NIKKI:

She was rushed to a CT scan. Along the way there, she fell into a coma.

Rob and I waited...and waited...and waited for what seemed like an eternity.

A nurse finally came and told us Aidan had some sort of mass on the front of her left side of the brain. *What? What did she just say?*

She said Aidan could die, or *would* die, if she was not rushed into surgery.

She was going to be airlifted to Cardon Children's Medical Center.

What? *What?*

We stood there, helpless, confused, scared, lost.

It just so happened that the father of a classmate of Aidan's was the lead nurse at the hospital. He gave us more information about what was happening, what was next.

He told us Aidan would be flown by helicopter to Cardon's for life-saving surgery. He told us to be prepared; she may not make it.

Rob wanted to fly with her, but because of the desert heat, there would be too much weight and so he was not allowed to go.

We were told to drive, calmly, to Cardon's and meet them there.

Did they just say CALMLY?

We hurried to our car and drove 9 miles from Banner Gateway to Cardon's.

I was losing my mind! What was happening? What was going on? Aidan! I was sobbing, angry, yelling and calm all at once.

We were pacing, waiting for her to arrive. Where was she? What was taking so long?

ROB:

We got to the hospital before the helicopter. We just stared at the landing pad. Where was our daughter? Then we saw the helicopter approaching, and my heart dropped. I'll never forget being at the landing pad and seeing our daughter land in the helicopter.

Aidan was pulled out of the helicopter on the gurney. We were told again that her condition was very bad. They took her away from us.

NIKKI:

It helped that at Cardon's, the nurses were fast and competent and compassionate. The first doctor we spoke to was calm, clear and concise.

We were told that Aidan had a massive clot in her left frontal lobe and that the swelling in her brain was growing. They didn't know what had caused the clot; all they needed to do was to get in there and save her life!

We had a (very) quick moment to speak to her surgeon, Dr. David Moss. He explained that he would do everything he could to save Aidan's life, but that it didn't look promising. He gave about a 3 percent chance of surviving.

ROB:

We were told again, "Your daughter may die. We will do everything we can to save her life, and she may die. We may save her life, and in the surgery our goal is to save her life. We are not doing anything else to help her with her potential brain damage and the consequences of that."

One of the scariest parts of the situation was actually having to say a temporary goodbye to our daughter as she was in the hospital bed on the way to surgery.

I didn't know if I'd see her alive again.

I remember it very clearly. I leaned close to Aidan and I looked into her eyes and said, "Aidan, you fight. You fight. Fight like your life depends on it. There are hundreds of thousands of people that need to meet you. There's a reason you're on this earth, and it is not your time to go. There are so many people that need to meet you. You fight. You continue to fight. Your job now is to fight. I love you, Aidan. Your mom and I are here for you. We're here for you. You fight. We love you. Go fight."

NIKKI:

And then we waited............

We called friends to come and be with us. We asked for prayers and love and prayers and more prayers.

We sat in the "quiet room" (which wasn't quiet at all) and waited. A nurse came in and let us know that surgery had started and that it would last several hours. She would keep us posted. Keep us posted...on what...whether our 14-year-old daughter had lived or died? I was frantic!

That nurse did come in, twice, to let us know that Aidan was doing okay.

Then Dr. Moss came in.

When I saw this man, the man whose hands were just in our daughter's brain, I nearly threw up.

What was happening? What was he here to say?

I held my breath.

ROB:

I remember thinking, *There's no way this is happening. There's no way. There's no way this is happening. This is not real.*

I'm pretty sure the worst thing that could happen to anybody is being told that their child may die.

Honestly, I was pinching myself, trying to wake up from this nightmare.

Then we got word that Aidan was doing well in surgery.

NIKKI:

Dr. Moss told us that Aidan had a blood clot the size of an orange explode in her brain. He told us that she had so much swelling that he thought her brain would implode.

IMPLODE!?

He told us that she had had four strokes in total.

He told us that she was alive but to be prepared because, even though she had made it through the surgery, she would probably stroke out in the next twelve hours.

What?

So the clock started ticking...

ROB:

She was on a ventilator, in a coma, but she was alive. Nikki and I kicked into hyper action mode and began to focus on all the things we needed to do to make Aidan's stay there as comfortable as possible.

We watched the minutes tick by, and after a full hour passed, we took a deeper breath. For the next seventy-two hours, we were mentally prepared for her to have another stroke and die. It was horrific. Every hour, the doctors and nurses would try to prepare us for her possible death.

NIKKI:

When we finally got to see our beautiful girl, she had a large bandage on the shaved part of her head. She was connected to a ventilator and hooked up to more than twenty tubes, wires, IV's. She was quiet and still and ALIVE.

I leaned in and told her I loved her, that she was a fighter. I told her that she was my world and that she brings all the color into it. I asked her to fight. I asked her to stay alive.

I watched that clock as if my life, and Aidan's life, depended on it.

The twelve hours came and went. ALIVE.

Then came the next forty-eight hours...these were the most crucial.

I cursed that clock; I begged it to hurry up and then I asked it to slow down. I wanted every moment I could have with my girl.

I talked to her, I sang to her, I prayed, I begged and I sat and watched as this amazing young soul lay quiet and still.

The forty-eight hours came and went. ALIVE.

AIDAN:

I could hear everything that my mom and dad were saying. They were telling me what day it was, what was happening, and every day they would come and ask me to open my eyes. I knew that my dad's birthday was coming up and I didn't have a present, so I wanted to open my eyes for him.

NIKKI:

On June 11, Rob's birthday, Aidan woke up.

I had begged her to open her eyes every day, to show me those soft brown eyes. And there they were.

She was confused and angry. I was happy and scared.

The next few days we were bombarded with information from the staff. They told us what would happen next. What kind of condition Aidan's brain was in. Etcetera, etcetera. We had plenty of questions of our own. Like, was she the same "Aidan" that we knew?

Side note: I have to take a moment to say some words about all of the nurses that were with us throughout all of this. These women are some of the best humans in the universe. Not only did they help me navigate all the medical jargon, they were the shoulder to lean on at 2 a.m. when I was certain I couldn't take another minute of it. They took such loving care of Aidan, of me. They will never really know what they did for us. I will forever love them.

As the days progressed, Aidan became more and more feisty, angry.

She wanted to know why this was happening to her.

I knew my girl was in there...we just needed to help her find a way to get back out!

Aidan had no use of her right side and was having a hard time swallowing. She couldn't speak.

Then, on June 16, Aidan spoke.

It was just a couple little words, but they were the most beautiful words I could ever hear.

AIDAN:

After they removed the tube from my throat, they kept asking me to talk. I knew Father's Day was coming up, and again, I didn't have a present, so I waited until Father's Day to speak. My first words were, "I love you, Daddy."

ROB:

Talk about the most amazing Father's Day gift I could ever ask for. She woke up, and she spoke! I don't think anything can ever top how I felt in that moment.

NIKKI:

The days went on, and Aidan got stronger. Therapists came and went.

Physical therapy helped her regain her strength.

She was determined.

Occupational therapy helped her regain some independence.

She was determined.

Speech therapy helped her find her words.

She remained...determined.

Massage therapy relaxed her tight muscles, eased her pain.

Music therapy soothed her soul.

Dog therapy put a smile on her face.

There were still so many questions. She was still confused as to why this happened to *her*.

Therapies took their toll. Emotions ran high. Frustrations were many.

On June 22, Aidan went to in-patient therapy at Rhodes Rehab Institute at Banner Baywood Medical Center. I moved into Rhodes Rehab Institute with her. We were told that she would be there for several weeks, possibly months. We were ready for the long haul. The unknown was scary. There were a lot of tears, and anger.

Aidan worked harder than I had ever seen her work. She was determined.

AIDAN:

Giving up was never an option for me. They would tell me I would be there for three months of rehab, and I got out in a week. My support group was my inspiration. My dad and my mom and my friends were with me every single day.

NIKKI:

On June 28, Aidan went home.

Aidan did such a remarkable job at rehab that they sent us home.

And that's when the fear set in! Were we really ready? Could I give her all that she needed at home?

I needed a shower chair and a hand-held shower. I needed a bell.

I needed...

When it came down to it, I needed my girl! I got my girl...and she was coming home!

On July 1, Aidan started out-patient therapy.

Here we go!

Aidan had a physical, occupational and speech therapy session four days a week for four hours a day.

She was so very determined.

We had an amazing therapy team. They were just as determined as Aidan was to get her back to her 14-year-old self. They were creative and compassionate and fun, and tough and loving too.

We will forever be grateful for and love them.

Aidan set a goal at the beginning of therapy: she WOULD start her freshman year of high school with the rest of her class on August 8.

And she did.

On August 8, Aidan started high school.

ROB:

After her rehabilitation, Aidan suffered from seizures, and they were bad, and frequent. As a matter of fact, the fire department knows the code to our front door, they were there so often. The ongoing care of Aidan became our top priority.

There's one more thing I want to add to this story. Not only did Aidan survive and thrive through brain surgery, thirty-six staples in her skull, four massive strokes, she also had to learn how to walk and talk again, as well as how to integrate using the right side of her body with the left. She is now this incredible, beautiful, magical 18-year-old girl, engaged to be married the year of this writing.

The journey wasn't easy. Unfortunately, my marriage to Nikki ended, but we have remained strong allies and advocates for Aidan.

Thankfully, we divorced amicably. Aidan was with each of us half the time, and I was so focused on making sure my daughter was okay that I let my own wellbeing slide. Luckily, when I didn't pay attention to what was happening to me, Aidan did.

I was working out religiously at the time, and I started noticing this incredible pain in my leg. I thought it was a charley horse, my calf was hurting so bad.

Aidan and I both knew that I had this blood clotting disorder called Factor V Leiden, but I had never had a blood clot.

The doctors decided since I didn't have a blood clot, I didn't need to be on a blood thinner. I didn't think about it anymore, and I definitely didn't associate it with the "charley horse" in my right leg.

I kept telling Aidan about this charley horse that was bugging me, and she wanted me to take action and go see a doctor.

I was so focused on her recovery and making sure she was okay, I didn't go. Nikki and I were on high alert all the time because Aidan would have these long seizures, so I just tried to fix it on my own. I rubbed my leg. I went and got deep tissue massage. I did all kinds of things to that leg because of my "charley horse." I thought I was taking action, but it was not the correct action. It wasn't until later that I discovered that "simply" taking the wrong actions could have killed me.

For months and months and months, Aidan kept telling me, "Dad, you have to go to the doctor. Dad, go to the doctor."

I was stubborn. I was so sure it was just a charley horse, because it came and went. Well, one night, it was proven to me that I did not have a charley horse.

My leg had swollen up, and felt like it was on fire.

I went to the ER, and they immediately did an ultrasound.

While the tech was doing it, she tried not to react, but I could tell something was very wrong. I asked her, "What's going on?" and she faked a smile and said the doctor would review my results.

At that point, I was overwhelmed with emotion and became very scared, mostly because nothing was supposed to happen to me. I am Aidan's father, and I am here to protect her, so I had to be okay. The way the tech acted told me it was serious. It was not just a "charley horse."

They wheeled me back into the ER room, and the doctor gave me morphine for the pain. He proceeded to explain that I had Deep Vein Thrombosis, or DVT. I had a blood clot, and I was very close to dying.

After looking at the ultrasound, the doctor looked at me and said, "It's a good thing you made it here, because you most likely would have died within an hour."

Because of my inaction, I have a blood clot, which you might imagine as a little speck in your blood vessel, but mine goes from the top of my thigh down to my ankle. Because I was not taking the proper action all this time, this sludge of blood had started forming in my leg.

All that inaction and incorrect action made the problem much worse. When I told the vascular surgeon that I had avoided coming in, he said, "Do you know how quickly you could've died if even a small part of the clot broke free, went through the vein, and into your heart or lungs? You would've died a very slow, unhappy death, or at the least have suffered a major stroke."

I was reminded many times that I could have died.

Your life can change in an instant. It did for my daughter. It did for me. Because I didn't take action, I was given a very clear message from my body, and the universe as well. I had to lie in bed for three months with my leg elevated throughout the day and night. Going from constant motion to suddenly not being physically able to do *anything* was incredibly frustrating. I had things to do, but I was on morphine for the first week and told to stay in bed as much as possible the rest of the time so the clot wouldn't break loose and end up killing me.

The silver lining was that it gave me time to think about taking action versus not taking action.

I was alone. I was scared. It was made very clear to me than even though I was following doctor's orders, there was still a chance that a small piece of the clot could break free, travel into my heart or lungs and cause a stroke that would end my life.

After watching my daughter almost die and go through the struggles she went through, I knew I had to fight to stay alive. It is my job to be there for Aidan.

I didn't listen to her when I should have, and I felt really dumb, scared and 100 percent committed to do whatever it would take to stay alive.

Recovery meant my life stopped. I couldn't work out, box, or do muay thai. Other than taking Aidan to school and picking her up, I spent three months resting.

During that time, I had a tremendous amount of time to think. I actually wrote this book, *The Law of Action*, in my mind. As I was lying in bed with my leg up, it was very quiet, and my brain played movies. It played the story of my life. I watched periods of inaction and times of action, and the differences were made very clear to me. That's where I came up with what is now the book, *The Law of Action*.

I started to see the consequences of not taking action. My inaction on taking care of my leg nearly killed me, but once I survived I was then faced with the need to be on medication and wear compression socks for the rest of my life. Not to mention the fact that I almost died.

Now I wear these stupid compression socks every day. They're not sexy, trust me, but guess what? If I don't take the action to put them on religiously every single day, I could get another DVT and possibly die. Talk about a good reason to take action.

I also have to take blood thinner medication every single day. Do you know what it's like to have to take a pill every day? Some of you do, some of you don't, but it sucks.

I've been told that I have to continue taking this pill every single day for as long as I live.

Taking action is not always fun, but it's necessary. It's not always easy, but it's worth it.

 Take a moment, and pause.

Things to think about:

- What are you avoiding in your life?

- What do you not do for yourself because you are too focused on others?

- What can you decide to do TODAY to make changes to these things using the Law of Action?

Chapter 2

IT'S NOT EASY, BUT IT'S WORTH IT

"It was character that got us out of bed, commitment that moved us into action, and discipline that enabled us to follow through."

-ZIG ZIGLAR

"If you don't take action, someone else will."

-ROB ACTIS

HAVE YOU EVER BEEN ON A PLANE, WAITING to take off, and it just drives on the jetway for what seems like FOREVER? You wonder, "Are we going to drive to my destination or are we actually going to fly?"

In life, "flying" would be taking action. Life is better when you actually take off the ground and fly. Like I tell my coaching clients, you need to live your life like you *want* to be alive.

Before I get any further, I want to share this story.

I've flown in airplanes all my life, but I recently attempted to check off something pretty awesome from my bucket list.

Do you have a bucket list? One thing on mine has always been to fly in a helicopter. Problem is I have a terrible fear of heights, which I've been working on over the past year or so. I know it is unreasonable, but my mind sure messes with me when I am over three feet off the ground.

Recently, when I was on the big island of Hawaii for a business trip, I got really excited to go on a helicopter and see the beauty of the island from a different perspective. The Decide part of the Law of Action was done; I decided it was time to do it. I was going to cross off "ride in a helicopter" off my bucket list. Wow.

On to Plan.

I picked up brochures for the only two helicopter tour companies in the area. When I looked over them, the reality of what I had decided to do hit me. My unreasonable fear of heights started to kick in right there with my feet still on the ground. I was imagining how beautiful the volcanoes and waterfalls would be from up high, but then I found myself visualizing some not-so-good scenarios. Yep, I was stuck in the planning stage, and fear was fighting with me. I had already asked my girlfriend, Tanya, if she was up for the helicopter trip, and she had said, "Hell yes!"

This was getting a bit too real for me. My mind was racing. I really did NOT want to do this. But how could I back out when she was all excited and had even said hell yes? Okay, now I had done it. Subconsciously, I was hoping that she would come up with a good reason to not do it so I could feel like I had made an attempt, and Tanya had put the brakes on the plan. Obviously, that didn't work. As she got more excited, I was getting much less excited. I knew this was an unreasonable fear, though, and I was starting to really get irritated with myself. I stood in a line full of families to get tickets. Even the kids were excited to go on the helicopter. I sucked it up and bought the tickets. I was taking action; now all I had to do was actually get into the helicopter the next day.

As we drove in the next morning, I watched the helicopters taking off. OH MY... I checked in, feeling really nervous. I knew it was put up or shut up, and I was not there yet. Interestingly, I was fully aware that the process was about moving through fear. I decided that I wanted to see the beautiful areas of Hawaii. I wanted to see the waterfalls and volcanoes from a different perspective. Tickets in hand, I stood there, determined to push through my fear of heights.

By then I was past the Plan part of the Law of Action and about to take Action. Though I was close, I couldn't consider this action complete until the helicopter took off with me in it. Many of us get so focused on the planning stage that we don't actually complete the actions needed to move us forward. Other times, we let fear stand in the way of taking action. Is that what you're doing in your life? Are you not acting, or are you stuck in planning?

Back to the helicopter trip. My mind raced. I took a few deep breaths, got centered and focused my thoughts. I told myself:

I'm going to do this.

I'm going to push through my fear because it's an unreasonable fear.

I get it. It's a helicopter that flies people every day, but it doesn't feel comfortable for me, and I understand that life is not always comfortable.

I can push through the discomfort and have an amazing experience.

When I follow the Law of Action, I move through the fear into joy. So let's see what happens next.

I was feeling better after re-centering myself, and then we got called into a room for the safety talk.

If I hadn't taken the time to focus my thoughts, what happened after that might have pushed me over the edge.

The safety video showed the usual things you'd expect, but then they talked about the automatic floatation devices that will activate in the event of a water landing. It retriggered my fear, and I started imagining the helicopter spinning out of control, making a crash landing in the ocean and the floatation devices activating. My subconscious mind was really starting to mess with me.

The staff member walked back in and said it was time.

So much conflict; at the same time that I felt really excited, I was still not confident I would be able to step onto the helicopter. I was doing everything in my power to push through some very unreasonable fear.

There were a couple of excited kids—I'm guessing eight to ten years old—nearby, which did not help my anxiety. But I was completely committed to getting on the helicopter, knowing it would be a life-changing moment. Overcoming my fear and getting on that helicopter would be a rite of passage, that's how big it felt.

As we walked toward the helipad, the sound of the chopper blades made the reality set in hard. I was surprised by how small the choppers were up close; I personally thought they would be much bigger.

I walked hand in hand with my fear and climbed into the helicopter. Here we go. OK...I was in the helicopter, and my stress level skyrocketed.

The kids were doing fine and I knew the fear was all in my head, but it stuck with me and freaked me out.

I didn't want to do it. I went back to focusing my thoughts.

It would be so freaking awesome to land on the other side of this fear, I knew.

My heart felt like it was racing a million miles a minute, so I thought about the volcanoes and other beautiful sights you don't see from the ground. At the same time the anxiety and fear sat with me, I held onto the little part that knew my life would be better and bigger. Transformed. I was pumped up; we were so close. Almost there. *Holy crap.*

After we got in the helicopter, they handed us a pair of headphones to put on. No joke, when I put them over my ears, I heard the song "Hallelujah"...Oh, great..I had angels singing in my ears. I thought, "Oh dear God, please God, tell me this is not a sign."

I began to really freak out inside, my anxiety level shooting through the roof. My mind was racing.

Captain Shawn said we were ready...

Yeah, I was *not.*

At that moment, it took everything in my power to stay on the helicopter. The words, "I really need to get off this helicopter, *now,*" almost came out of my mouth. I thought to myself, "I am not a quitter, and I do not often get stuck in the planning stage and give up. That's not me; that is not how I live my life."

I took a deep breath and knew that after I pushed through that enormous fear, my ability to move through other things that were holding me back would be forever changed.

I embraced the fear, took another deep breath, and really soaked in the experience of what was to follow and the feeling of accomplishment that I would feel after we landed.

And then we took off.

The chopper lifting into the air was a very moving experience for me. I didn't feel completely okay right away, but I had made the decision to enjoy the beautiful experience, so I fully embraced all of it. I allowed the sounds and the views and the feeling inside to completely take over. I surrendered.

A few minutes into the flight, we were pretty high and I was okay; I felt surprisingly at peace. I had just overcome my fear of heights in a huge way.

The views were really spectacular. We flew over jungles and waterfalls and an active volcano with flowing molten lava. From up there, we could see how lava had covered miles of beaches. It was an unforgettable experience. I'm not sure I could have forgiven myself if I had missed it.

When we landed, I was actually disappointed that it was over. I felt so empowered, and remarkably calm. Almost a Zen-like feeling.

The Law of Action was complete again, and all I felt was peace. Calm. Just...fantastic.

I checked "ride in a helicopter" off my bucket list and actually got excited about the idea of taking helicopter tours in other places.

After overcoming that fear that I'd had for many years, I felt pretty much invincible and wondered what my next challenge would be. I now feel like I can accomplish anything. *Anything.* That FEAR tried so hard to stop me, but in the end I knew it was just "False Expectations Appearing Real."

Being able to conquer my fear of heights allowed me an experience I will never forget. The Law of Action is simple enough for anyone to learn, and powerful enough to change your life in every moment.

Decide, Plan, Act. That's it.

As you read through this book, you'll be reminded of those three words of the Law of Action. You'll be reminded a lot, because that's the best way for it to stick in your mind. Creating new habits takes time, awareness, and repetition.

It's not easy, but it's worth it.

(Have you ever heard that saying?)

A lot of people plan and over-prepare for things but never end up actually DOING anything. Fear blocks them from taking action, even though it is the most critical step of the Law of Action.

The most important part is to ACT! Otherwise, you can end up planning forever and never getting anywhere.

Clue in to the Success of Others

I have learned in life to pay attention, because success leaves clues. I have also learned that watching other people succeed, especially noticing their work ethic and who they are as a person, can help me in my roadmap to success.

I have been watching someone who takes massive action, and in a big way. I have said to myself many times that if I can just be one-fourth as productive as this man, Mike Koenigs, that would be an amazing accomplishment. I came across Mike while watching a video online about seven years ago. His energy and passion for others really drew me to him. There was something that he said that I think would have almost sounded dumb or self-serving if it had been said by someone else, . But when I heard Mike say that he wanted to create one million millionaires, I believed he could do it. That was a pretty bold statement, but I genuinely believed him. I purchased his various programs and did not see the success that others saw. The programs were step-by-step. I can't blame anyone but myself for my lack of success. I decided I wanted to do it, I planned to do it, but I never really took action. That is 100 percent on me.

It is amazing to me how people come in and out of your life, and you really do not know why. I met Mike in person at one of his big events, and the one thing that I remember about him is that he has a big heart.

At the end of 2017, I was fortunate to cross paths with Mike again. A lot had changed in my life since the last time I saw him. This time, it was not a quick meet and greet. I actually had a chance to hang out with and get to know him.

I was able to reinforce my belief that he truly is an amazing human being. He is caring and genuinely wants to impact people's lives in such a positive way.

Yes, he is extremely successful in business; he not only founded and built Traffic Geyser Instant Customer, he was also the head of a team that generated many multi-million-dollar launches in a row. One hit almost ten million dollars.

On top of his success in business, he genuinely cares about others and giving back. He has contributed millions of dollars to his wife's charity, the Just Like My Child Foundation that supports women's education, entrepreneurial education, and legal education for kids in Uganda and Senegal.

As of this writing, Mike just celebrated five years of being cancer-free. He is a survivor of stage three colorectal cancer, which is absolutely brutal; he had four months of chemotherapy and over thirty-three laser treatments and survived. He's emerged more focused, more passionate and more alive, with a bigger mission than ever.

Mike Koenigs is the perfect example of someone who obeys the Law of Action. He decides he is going to do something, he makes a plan, then he takes massive, immediate action. And he goes through the steps very quickly. You might find this hard to believe, but he wrote and published the #1 international bestselling book, *Cancerprenuer*, in just two days! Now *that* is massive, immediate action.

When I talked to Mike about the Law of Action and told him about the three steps—Decide, Plan and Act—he agreed that there are so many people who have such amazing opportunity and just get stuck in the planning stage and never get to action.

Taking action can be a challenge, and learning to apply the Law of Action will ease you into taking those big, challenging steps by first getting comfortable with small steps.

Taking Action in Every Area of Your Life

As you will see throughout this book, you can apply the Law of Action to everything you do.

For example, I've got a background in network marketing. I've done it, and I've had both success AND failure with it. There are people who have had enormous success, and I watched and learned from them. That was a part of my success. I watched them Decide, Plan, and Act, and recognized that in myself.

"Hey, I DO THAT!"

Decide, Plan, Act *is* the Law of Action.

It translates into EVERY aspect of life. When you develop the self-discipline to continually follow the Law of Action, you can LITERALLY apply it to everything you do.

From the mundane to the magnificent things, just apply Decide, Plan, Act to EVERYTHING!

It's a way of thinking and awareness that will take time to get used to, but if I can use it all the time, so can you.

Check out this ridiculously simple example of using the Law of Action in everyday life.

Using the Law of Action to Get Dressed in the Morning

- **Decide** to get dressed for your day.

- **Plan** your clothing based on the day's activities, for example: *It's going to be a bit chilly, and I've got a client meeting, then lunch with a friend. The best thing to wear is, blah blah blah...*

- **Act** by getting dressed.

Seems silly, right? But...

What happens if you don't finish the cycle and act in that scenario? You spend your whole day standing in your closet, planning what to wear.

Our mind places value on things, but every concept can be scalable.

It's no different than this bigger example, which applies to network marketing.

Using the Law of Action to Join a New Company

- **Decide** that you really like this product line and the results it gives people. It is helping people feel better. You feel good about the people who are inviting you, and you'd like to work with them. Thinking about this brings you joy. You are excited!

- **Plan** to do some research and check your resources to make sure you have the time and money to spend on this opportunity. Go in prepared to act and create a business.

> - **Act** by becoming part of the team and devoting time to sharing and promoting this company and its products.

A lot of people get into network marketing hoping to make a bunch of money without considering the work it will take.

What happens? They fail. Sometimes they blame the company. The bottom line is they didn't take action on the right things.

Maybe they got invited in but spent so much time researching and preparing, they never actually joined the company? Remember, over-preparing is just as bad as over-planning.

People get caught up in thinking, *Before I act on this, I'm gonna read this book* or *I'm gonna write in this journal* or *I'm gonna listen to this podcast* or *I'm gonna sit in on this webinar* or *I'm gonna look things over....* I'm gonna research about this, research about that...

It's INSANITY!

It's all busy work, delays and distractions! If you aren't sure about acting on something, maybe it isn't for you.

That's okay too.

Sometimes taking action IS deciding to stop moving toward something. Then you can gather your energy and redirect it to something else you decide to do.

And once you know you *want* to do something, take action. One of my favorite quotes from Napoleon Hill is, "Don't wait. The time will never be just right."

It won't! Instead of planning and planning and *planning*, you HAVE to do the whole cycle.

Decide, Plan, Act. Oh, here's another thing: lists.

Do you make lists? They are a very common way of over-preparing, BUT they can be effective when used as a tool and not an avoidance.

Here's a way to use lists effectively.

Using the Law of Action to Create Beneficial Lists

- **Decide** what the list is for; limit it to a single project or put a short time frame on it with a specific deadline (preferably in the near future).

- **Plan** the result before making the list. Think about the desired outcome, and imagine it is complete. Imagine the steps to get there.

- **Act** by writing the topic at the top of the list, then write steps SPECIFIC to the plan in a logical order. Look at your list, knowing the end result, and feel the joy of completing it, then take action and finish it!

Lists should only be used for SMALL projects. When you try to use a list for a large project, it can quickly get overwhelming, and unless you are really good at organizing your processes, the overwhelm can be paralyzing. If you do have large projects on your plate, try chunking them down into a series of smaller projects to be tackled one at a time. So, let's avoid overwhelm by breaking things down. Good project managers begin with the end in mind. Before starting, they look at the desired result, then they reverse engineer it. Let's talk about the reverse engineering process for a minute. I like really amazing sandwiches, so let's reverse engineer one as an example.

When the thought of making a sandwich is terrifying.

People don't take action because they're scared. Perception is such a big part of this. Is making a sandwich SCARY to you? Likely not. Why is that?

Because it's a small project. The steps are simple and can be quickly completed.

People don't think that they can accomplish the task at hand when it's a big task, but they can if they break it down. Making a sandwich and building a business, for example, both take the same steps; one is just repeated more often. What are those steps again?

Decide, Plan, Act.

Anyone can do anything! You will be amazed when you take action. You decide that you want something. You make the plan, and then act on it.

Decide, Plan, Act. It's as easy as making a sandwich.

Using the Law of Action to Reverse Engineer a Sandwich

- **Decide:** Close your eyes and imagine the finished sandwich in your hands. It's been neatly cut in half, so you can see all of

---

the layers in it. What sort of bread do you use? Is it toasted? What's inside the sandwich? What condiments are on it?

- **Plan:** Now that you know what the sandwich looks like, get out the ingredients you need for your sandwich. If you are missing something, find a substitute, and maybe add it to a grocery list (which is a great use for a list, by the way).

- **Act:** Build your sandwich. The bread is the outer layer, right? The mayo (or peanut butter, mustard, etc.) get spread with a spoon or knife on the inside of the bread. These things seem so simple, we do them all the time without thinking. Next comes the lettuce, roast beef, ham, salami, provolone cheese, pickles, tomato, pesto, olives, feta cheese...whatever your sandwich needs, put it in the right order.

Just like that, you've gone from hungry to holding a delicious sandwich in hand, ready to devour. Same thing goes for anything you want in life. Decide what you want it to look like, plan out your steps, and then take action.

So. What are you waiting for? Remember, the time will never be just right. You might fail, but the best part about taking action is that you're *allowed* to fail. You probably won't put the mayo on the outside of the bread more than once, because it makes the sandwich slippery and messy to hold. You learned, though, right? Failure doesn't have to be this huge, terrifying thing. Just learn from your mistakes, and go back to Decide, Plan, Act.

It's all about moving forward, getting closer and closer to your goal.

Decide, Plan, Act.

By the end of this book you will remember the Law of Action and hopefully implement it into your life. The three main steps are the core of the cycle, but there's more!

After Act is Observe, then Repeat.

What do you do when you fail? How do you feel? Let's explore something. Imagine you just finished a Decide, Plan, Act cycle and FAILED miserably. Enormously, in fact. You are devastated and almost ready to give up.

The aftermath is here, and you can let it shut you down, or you can use a mini cycle to get you back in gear.

Using the Law of Action for Failures

- **Decide** that you are okay, because failure is part of success. Forgive yourself! Maybe step away for a bit, and let the emotion subside so you can get clear again.

- **Plan** to understand the failure's purpose and open yourself to be humble enough to get it. At the same time, decide not to make the same mistake again.

- **Act** by adjusting and retrying OR abandoning the thing you failed at and trying something new. In either case, go back to Decide.

There. Back in the saddle.

Failure makes you better. People fail. We all fail. The people that you consider successful are those who didn't let their failures stop them.

The Law of Action is a cycle, or circle. It's repeatable, and the more you repeat it, the more things will move in your life.

What's Your Speed of Action?

How fast do you move on a daily basis?

It will help if you accept YOUR speed! People operate at different speeds, so some will apply the Law of Action several times a day and others will apply it weekly, or even monthly. Everyone who does use it will use it differently, and that's all good. My lifelong experience has been that the most successful people move through Decide, Plan and Act the fastest. The bottom line is that massive, immediate action always wins. Because if you don't take action, someone else will.

The point is to keep going, and don't get stuck.

When I continually repeat "Decide, Plan, Act" in this book, I am intending to create movement for your life. We all know repetition is a great way to learn, so let's fill our databases with the good stuff.

It's really a mindset and a thought pattern which can help if you let it. It's the kind of brainwashing that you need. It eliminates that other stuff that keeps you stuck.

Even though all this action is a great thing for many people, maybe you are someone who moves more slowly. You might not be a massive action taker... yet. But the fact that you're reading this book tells me you are capable of getting there, so don't give up!

This can all seem overwhelming at first, so take it in and allow it to get into your mind. Oh yes, the mind...capable of creating anything, and infinitely creative. What do you feed your mind on a daily basis?

What do you tell yourself all day? Do you paralyze yourself with limiting thoughts that create inaction? Speaking of, let's visit our arch nemesis...

The Law of Inaction

What I've just called "the Law of Inaction" can't even be given recognition as a law; it's really just breaking the Law of Action. As far as it being an arch nemesis, I may be exaggerating, but not that much. There are two sides to everything. Balance, right? It's how the universe operates, so pretending the other side isn't there won't work. In general, I put my attention and awareness on what I *do* want, so I get more of that in my life. That being said, I'm still human, and I've certainly screwed up by not following the Law of Action when I really, *really* should have. In not following the Law of Action, I inadvertently followed the Law of INACTION. Oops.

I will say I'm good at failing, and I'm good at learning from failures. So there's that!

What Happens if You Break the Law of Action?

Breaking the Law of Action is just like breaking any other law; there are consequences.

The consequence could be painful. It could be physical pain, or financial pain. In one personal instance for me, it was both.

As someone who believes in the Law of Attraction, affirmations, and positive thinking, I think very often about having great teeth. I don't eat much candy or sugar. I work to take meticulous care of my teeth. I brush them plenty, however, I am not a very good flosser.

Not only am I not a regular flosser, but for some stupid reason, I recently discovered I hadn't gone to the dentist for the past nine months. When I finally went in, what happened as a result was both financially painful and just downright physically painful.

My inaction resulted in over four hours in the dentist's chair as they did extremely painful things to my gums because I hadn't been flossing. The bill when I was done was quite a shock, too. All of which could have been avoided (or at least lessened) if I'd simply flossed my teeth.

There are consequences from both action and inaction. Choosing to use the Law of Action keeps you moving consciously through your life.

On that note, I want to share an interview with a good friend of mine, Brian Anderson.

ROB:

So, Brian, you have been an entrepreneur all your life, right?

BRIAN:

Oh yeah, I would go around with my lawn mower and my younger brother, and we would cut yards for $5 in the front and $10 in the back. It was big money in the early '80s. I was always in the mindset of making a few extra bucks. When I worked for any company, I always had small side projects going on. I always looked for something to create.

ROB:

All right, I'm going to change the tone here a bit. I'm a huge fan of your companies, Voice Drops and Media Mash, so I know you're wildly successful now. What I want to know first is about when you failed. Tell me when you took action and failed, or didn't take action and lost an opportunity.

BRIAN:

All right, Rob. You asked for it.

It's 1994. I'm in grad school at Notre Dame, second-year MBA student. I don't know a lot of people. So, what do I do? AOL. This is early, early, early internet. I created an info product in Word Perfect and launched it on AOL.

Wait until you hear how this went. I built this product in the relationship dating space. It sold for $20. I made on average $200 or $300 a day, the whole time I was in school. These payments would literally come in as checks over the internet, and every morning I would wake up and print them out. It was unbelievable, Rob, but I made it happen. I had the force of will, and the follow-through to deliver, but guess what?

I let it languish. I got distracted. I just...never followed up on it. I never grew that business. That entrepreneurial pursuit was sitting in front of me, and instead I went into a miserable corporate existence where I travelled all the time. I was away from my family. I gained weight and became extremely unhealthy. I went from 5'10", 180 pounds and in fairly good shape to 5'10", 235 pounds and in miserable shape. I was married and had a horrible work life in terms of travel and always being gone.

Thinking back, if I had really lived the Law of Action and grown this amazing product in 1994, which really pre-dates almost everything online, I never would have been in the corporate world or had those challenges. I may have been a very influential and popular marketer in the late '90's, but it never happened. Why? Because I failed to take action.

The space filled up with a lot of legends who we all know. Ryan Deiss, Frank Kern, Matt Bacak, and lots of others. A lot of internet marketers bloomed in the late '90's.

ROB:

Brian, wow, thanks for sharing that because so many people see successful people and think they have it easy. I just want to throw this at you, as a question. How much do you think, as an estimate, did not taking that action cost you? Aside from the life path and physical health issues, I mean in actual dollars?

BRIAN:

So from 1994, let's just say—and this is still a conservative number—that I got a half a million a year. Over fourteen years, that's seven million dollars. I'd like to think I would have grown far beyond that but the reality is, I probably lost five to ten million dollars of real money, plus the freedom of time, happiness, and the ability to live a healthier lifestyle.

I can trace it back to that time in grad school, when I chose complacency and instead of following my real dream and acting on my passion, I chose to follow the status quo. It took having my wife leave me to jolt me in a lot of areas and push me to redefine myself.

I knew I had to be my own boss and an entrepreneur, whether I made millions of dollars or $50,000. I knew that happiness wasn't defined by how much money I made but by freedom of time to spend with my family and do things that I enjoyed.

Thinking about having an extra seven million really doesn't matter because more important than any of the money was the feeling of self-worth and purpose that I lost because I chose to become a victim of my own complacency.

ROB:

Did you feel unworthy of a happy life?

BRIAN:

Yeah...and one day, Rob, I hit rock bottom. I was divorced, my wife had left me. Even as amiable as it was, she left me and the reality was I knew I had to make a change. I had to choose better for myself. I started working out twice a day and eating the way I knew was healthy. It was all a choice. I used to eat pizzas late at night with Oreo cookies and Diet Coke. No more. I switched. I started eating healthy, and in less than six months, Rob, forty pounds dropped off of me. *Forty pounds.* I don't wanna tell you it's because I was a workout king; I just changed my choices.

When I found myself getting ready to cheat, I would drink more water. I was so committed, and I was in love with the results I was getting. This isn't hard. It doesn't matter what you do. If you follow the Law of Action, you're gonna get results because the path is clear, but most people just choose not to follow it.

ROB:

So, then you chose the path you are on now; how do you feel?

BRIAN:

Great! Even though it took major life events—getting laid off and getting divorced—to jolt myself to do what I already knew. I decided, I planned, and I acted, and the results were unbelievable. No more double or triple chin. I'm not a fitness star, but you know what, I'm happy with how I look and feel. It means a lot to be able to set a good example for my kids. I'm remarried now, and I have three daughters and a son.

ROB:

Then you became an actual entrepreneur? What did that look like?

BRIAN:

From 2009 on, I have been a 100 percent full-time entrepreneur. I currently have a company called Media Mash. We're based in Peachtree City, Georgia, just outside of Atlanta. We service a few hundred accounts in the area, providing digital marketing solutions and strategy for small businesses.

By 2011, I was running Media Mash, a seven-figure marketing agency, as well as a seven-figure information publishing business where I would create content and strategy and teach other marketers how to be successful and how to take the next step in their entrepreneurial pursuits. That has grown and progressed over the last nine years.

Now, I focus more on the software side in supporting other entrepreneurs. I'm building tools and resources that give them an edge over their competition. I also speak at a lot of events in the U.S. and abroad. That's been my journey. I started off a hungry kid growing up in a military family, with divorced parents, who just wanted to make a few extra bucks to grab a slice of pizza and go play video games. I worked hard through school and realized "a great job" was just a myth. There's no loyalty in the corporate world. You have to have portable skills and be loyal to yourself and your family. When you do that, then you're highly valued. You'll never be out of work or hurt for income. You'll be able to grow. Now, I run two businesses: a company called Voice Drops and Media Mash, mentioned earlier.

ROB:

You've definitely taken action to get where you are. What is the best part about your life and owning two successful businesses?

Brian:

You know what? It's freedom and free time. I enjoy a lot of quality time with my wife, Rebecca, and my four kids. I also was elected to the school board in our county. I'm one of the five elected officials that control a $200 million school budget. It just gave me a new challenge. I was hungry for something more. Somebody asked, "Why would you do it?"

I said, "Well, I have time." I have freedom of time. I have freedom of income, and I really do want to make a difference and help. It was an area that I always was interested in. In another world, I could see myself being a teacher, a high school teacher, and challenging kids and inspiring them. This gave me a chance to intersect my passion for helping others and the community, and being involved where my kids are. It gave me a chance to support the school system in doing the right thing.

ROB:

Creating income isn't a challenge for you. You've shown up to do the work and have great results to show for it.

BRIAN:

Yeah, I grew one business, a texting platform, and it blew my mind. I would make this money, $75,000 in less than five days, all with email. That literally opened my eyes, but I realized something. To keep the income coming, I would have to do more new work, create something amazing and fresh, and then earn some money.

Sometimes I'd make a quarter million, but I knew there had to be a way to deliver value to my customers, where I would get a recurring payment, whether it was monthly or periodically, and I could deliver immense value to the customer. I took this texting platform, and it had a bunch of other apps and cool features, and I ended up building a seven-figure, recurring business that I kept for about three years, until I sold it.

Now, you might think, "Wow, amazing!" and I agree, so after I sold it, I had to create something new. So I asked myself, "What's the number one problem that my customers have which I could solve?"

So, in 2013 and the early part of 2014, I worked on creating a new software, which is now called Voice Drops. Voice Drops was a way to market to your targeted audience without ever calling them, emailing them, or doing anything that would put a potential customer in an awkward position, so what Voice Drops does is deliver the voicemail message directly to the customer's voice mail. It's great! If I sent 100 messages to 100 prospects for one of my customers, they would get maybe 10-15 calls back, resulting in qualified conversations to help build their businesses.

I was charging $200 a month, and I was hoping to sign up 50 accounts. The first week, Rob, I think I signed up 300 accounts, and I currently have over 3,000 members using Voice Drops. It's a fabulous software system that delivers value and results to my clients, while also building a recurring revenue for me. I would say that in my entrepreneurial history, this has been my greatest success.

Now I've created this income stream for myself, my family, and my future that is a sellable asset, and guess what? It makes money each and every day, whether I'm creating anything new or not, which was the challenge I knew I needed to overcome.

I knew I wanted to go beyond information products and increase the value of my service and product to my customer. I had to go down that path, so next, I had to plan. I spent a year and a half, almost, planning, strategizing, and developing out the exact system.

I had a small team, five employees, and when I was leading this team, all of us took massive action. We used webinars, email, and even video—which I wasn't very good at, but I did it anyway—to help me sell. I met my customers wherever they were, and the platform is still growing today. I've added more features and functionality. I think you can never stop following Decide, Plan, Act. I have definitely learned not to become complacent.

ROB:

Thanks so much, Brian. You are such an inspiration, and so real about it all.

How do we keep ourselves motivated, though? The truth is that self-motivation is a SKILL! One that must be honed and developed. On top of that, most successful people have help. No, actually, *every successful person has help*!

I have learned that with action comes reward. I have learned that having help makes taking action flow more smoothly. Working alone takes a high level of self-motivation, which is great and all, but working with others allows mutual support and accountability, and that's really great stuff.

I want to tell you a story about an amazing fitness coach, Jason Kamens.

Jason is amazing.

I've known a lot of trainers, but Jason is different. He's a coach, and the difference is he pays attention to his client's unique needs and works with them where they are.

Jason coaches and trains professional athletes, like Ryan Bader, the Bellator Light Heavyweight Champion of the World. (He's an amazing athlete and MMA fighter, and you'll see an interview with him at the end of this chapter.)

Jason is also my fitness coach.

What I love about working with Jason, and being around these MMA fighters, is seeing how they take massive action. Their training is all about taking unbelievably massive action! They can't think, they have to react. If they don't, they get hurt, and they don't have a career.

Their commitment to action is explosive and fast. If you've ever watched these fighters, you know what I mean, but the next time there's a fight on, really watch it. If they lose focus for a split second, it can all be over.

Working with Jason keeps me accountable to my own fitness and health.

Jason pushes my limits, because he knows my limits better than I do. He doesn't accept failure, because he knows what I can do. There have been times in my workout when he has added weights, and I have no idea how much. I trust him. He never gives me anything I can't handle.

Another thing he does, which is really exciting, is take little steps. Not giant steps. This helps me get better, and better, and better. And as for "fitness," we focus not on my appearance but my health, my strength, and how I feel.

I've been successful working out this way. If I had gone to a gym and tried to work out alone, I probably would have overdone it, and then given up. Working with Jason has taught me consistency. At 53 years old, I'm in the great shape that I'm in because I am consistent. I work out with Jason two to three times a week, and I also work out at home. I know that if I don't do those things, I'm going to fall to the wayside and be back where I started.

Let's take a look at how the Law of Action has been helping me reach my health goals and how you can use this same technique to reach your health goals too.

Using the Law of Action for My Personal Fitness and Health

- **Decide** that I was ready to feel great, fit, and healthy. Imagine looking in the mirror and seeing a strong, lean version of myself.

- **Plan** to allow time to devote to my health and to connect with the right coach for me.

- **Act** by hiring Jason, showing up, and working out at home as well.

The results have been phenomenal. I'm in really good shape for a 53-year-old man, and I'm not saying that out of ego; I'm saying it's amazing. I was told that because of the changes I made to my physical fitness and health, that I actually lived a lot longer when I went through the experience with my blood clot. Being healthy probably saved my life in that instance.

I may not be a champion fighter, but I'm happy with how I feel and look. Working out alongside these guys inspires me to keep it going, but my coach meets me where I'm at. It's really cool.

That's how you know you have a great coach: they see your potential and keep pushing you to reach it. It's the same when I work with clients in my field. When I'm in the coaching role, I'm the expert, and I get to encourage and challenge my clients to reach their full potential the same way Jason coaches me.

Have you ever hired a personal trainer or fitness coach? Do you know what to ask them to determine if they are a good match for you?

I thought it would be helpful to have a chat with Jason and ask him to share a few tips on finding the perfect trainer for you based on where you are right now.

ROB:

Jason, as my fitness coach, you've helped me transform my body. You've pushed me in a way that has helped me tremendously. Can you share some thoughts on finding the right fitness coach for people who are looking to improve their overall strength and wellbeing?

JASON:

I have a solid foundation of principles which apply for anyone I might work with, so I'd say the first thing is to ask about their training and education. Continuing education means they are always learning and updating their knowledge base, and degrees are great; they show a dedication to learning. The National Strength Conditioning Association, the American College of Sports Medicine and the National Academy of Sports Medicine are the big three that should stand out when asking about their education. If they have a bachelor's degree and are certified as well, they meet pretty high standards. If they have a master's degree in one of those certifications, it's pretty much gold standard as far as a trainer can go on paper.

ROB:

Definitely. So what would the second thing be?

JASON:

Experience. It doesn't matter how much you know on paper or from books unless you've applied it and experienced it. Any good coach will openly share how long they have been at it. They need to have some years in the gym where they've spent time training different types of people with different backgrounds. They will be more effective if they have had to problem solve and figure out situations for people's unique needs.

ROB:

You are so great at that, Jason, how you shift coaching methods from me to Ryan Bader. You just get it.

JASON:

Yes, that would be the third thing.

A great coach can adapt to their client in any situation and be a problem solver. Sometimes it takes creativity and, of course, the client's feelings about the whole thing, to use different types of equipment, different exercises, etc. Find someone you like who actually listens to you.

ROB:

I had no idea working out could be so enjoyable. That has become a big deal for me. I actually enjoy our time. Okay, so what's the fourth thing?

JASON:

Professionalism. They have to be professional in communication, punctuality, and things like that. It's important to show that level of professionalism and customer service.

ROB:

Yes. I think these things carry across hiring any type of coach. I would hope my clients consider these things before hiring me. I want to be the best coach for them, but I know I'm not for everyone.

JASON:

Exactly. That's number five: ask about their niche. If you want a bodybuilding trainer, it wouldn't make sense to hire a sports performance coach. Ask for testimonials or referrals, or see if you can meet other clients.

ROB:

Perfect. Okay, so to recap. Five things to check on to match yourself with the best fitness coach for you:

1. Education

2. Experience

3. Adaptability

4. Professionalism

5. Niche

Moving right along, I want to introduce you to a friend of mine, Bellator Light Heavyweight Champion of the World, Ryan Bader.

I know you because we have the same trainer, and we cross paths that way. I know you're the Bellator Light Heavyweight Champion. In this book, I want to get to know you more by inviting you to share about how you have used the Law of Action to get where you are, but I want to know the real Ryan Bader. The stuff you went through and overcame.

RYAN:

For sure. My college wrestling career was one of the hardest things that I went through. Day in and day out, we were the wrestling team, the track team, and the swim team, because we did all of that. On Saturday mornings, we ran in the mountains. It was very strenuous and a big mental challenge, too.

I had a scholarship to Arizona State University. I did pretty well my freshman year, but in my sophomore year, I ranked number one in the country. At one point, I ended up getting fourth place in Nationals, and I was an All-American as a sophomore, which is a big deal.

I was riding that into my junior year. I wanted to become a national champion, because I had been wrestling my whole life. I felt a little burnt out, though. I was making the wrong choices, sabotaging myself.

I got in this mode where I was kind of being a front runner. If I wasn't up by five points, I would let the match slip away. I would try to do a big throw because I didn't want it to be close. I didn't want to have to fight for that one point that could have meant winning or losing a match.

Don't get me wrong, I was a good wrestler with a great record, but the first match of my junior year, I went out there and I lost.

I was making these choices where in my head I was like, "Oh, I'll get it back for sure."

The only tournament that matters is the national championships. That's where you become an All-American. So I was just going to show up for that. In my head, I kept telling myself I was doing the right thing, but deep down I knew I wasn't. I'd never drink any alcohol or anything during wrestling season, but that season my friends were all going to Spring Break. I figured, I can have a few beers, it's not going to hurt me, but I knew I wasn't doing the right things even when I was telling myself I was.

Going into the national tournament, I won my first match. All I had to do was win two more to be in the semi-finals. It got tough, and I really felt like I didn't want it that bad, so I gave that match away, and then another one. I was out of that tournament. I didn't get All-American. I went from fourth place in the country with the best guys to being left out. And that hurt. It was one of the lows in my wrestling career.

I had a coach who came to me at the middle of the season and told me to go back to where I'd win by one or two points. Winning is winning. And I said I would do that but found myself still doing that front runner stuff where I'd try to get big points and not just win the match.

ROB:

What do you think that mindset cost you?

RYAN:

It caused me mental stress for a year and a half, until the next NCAA tournament when I ended up All-American. It cost me confidence, and confidence is everything when you're going into an athletic career, you know? For me, it was my last year. I didn't place as a junior, and I went into my senior year thinking I couldn't do the same things as I did last year, but in the back of my head I was still not sure I was doing the right things. That whole year was just as stressful.

I remember that feeling when I knew I didn't give it my all and I lost. That's what ate me up the most. If I go out and give it my all, and I put everything on the mat or in the cage or whatever it is, I can live with myself if I lose. But if I didn't give everything out there and I lost, it would just eat at me. So it was a full year of that just eating at me. It probably messed with relationships I had because I was grumpy.

ROB:

Like a domino effect.

RYAN:

Exactly. It messes up everything, you know? Yeah, it's one part of your life, but at that time in my life I was a college student and I got a scholarship to go and wrestle at ASU, so I felt like I was letting not only myself down but also my team, my coaches, my family, everything. It was a huge domino effect, and I felt like I did it to myself.

ROB:

Wow. So you had your life mission. You decided to be a World Champion Fighter. You paid your dues, planned, trained, and took action. You made it to the UFC and had success, and then what happened?

RYAN:

I always wanted to be the best, at the top, the very pinnacle of the sport. That's really my drive in everything that I do. I don't want to be fourth, fifth, or sixth; I want to be first.

I was going into a mixed martial arts career. I was undefeated, 12-0 in the UFC, and ranked top ten after a few fights. I was ranked in the top five for a decade. I was beating top guys, there was nobody behind me that I hadn't beat. At one point, I had won my last five fights in the UFC, all against tough competition. I wanted a chance. I wanted an opportunity to get this title shot, and I kept at it, training as hard as I could to accomplish this goal. I called the UFC president, Dana White, introduced myself and pleaded my case. They had a fighter pull out of a fight, and I had an opportunity to jump in for the Light Heavyweight Championship with the UFC. Since I pleaded my case, it was kind of one of those things where they were like, *Look, go out there, win your next fight. We'll give you this title shot.*

I went out there, did everything in my power, and I won that fight. I still didn't get a title shot, so I had to sit down and say, "All right. If I'm not getting a title shot now, when will I ever get one? When will I get the opportunity to show that I'm the best in the world?"

I had to take action. I knew I had two fights left on my UFC contract, so I said to myself, "I'm just going to have fun with these fights. I'm gonna fight my contract out."

In the UFC, they're never going to let you be a free agent; they're always going to sign you when you have one fight left so you never can go play their contract against anybody else.

So I went out there, and I was being loose and happy. I knocked out my guy. Then I got a short-notice call to step into another fight in the UFC. Since I'd accepted a fight, I had the opportunity to fight out my contract. And so then a week later, they're like, "Yeah, we're going to have to sign a new deal with you."

I said, "Oh, yeah, I'm not going to do that. I'm going to fight my contract out." And they were super pissed that I fought out the contract, which, for any other sport, is just common business, but apparently not in the UFC.

The team of coaches, agents and I knew we were going to take some flak for that and it might mean not being able to return to the UFC, but we took those calculated risks. We reached out to Bellator, knowing what kind of contract they might offer. I was taking a risk going over to Bellator but we signed the contract anyway.

I was supposed to fight another tough guy named King Mo. He ended up pulling out, and they offered me a chance at the World Title against Phil Davis, who is arguably one of the top three guys in the world at this weight class. Not only that, it was also a fight at Madison Square Garden. I obviously accepted. I went in there and trained my butt off, knowing I had some obstacles I had to overcome. It was a stressful time. We had to find a place to train, but I wasn't going to let that get in the way of accomplishing my goal. I just kept my head down and said, "Get through this. You're going to win this title, and then all's going to be well and we'll just keep on rolling."

I went into that fight, excited. It was refreshing. I was in a new organization. It was big. The fight was at Madison Square Garden, like I said, and I had thirty friends and family with me when I accomplished a lifelong goal. It was a close fight, and then it all came down to those couple of words that he'd say at the very end that would end up being cumulation of your life's work. And there it was.

"Forty-eight, forty-seven..." And that feeling was a huge weight off my shoulders. I accomplished my goal.

I got that better contract and that belt wrapped around my waist, and it was the best feeling in the world.

ROB:

Bellator Light Heavyweight Champion of the World. Sweet.

RYAN:

Yep. Now I defend the belt, and not only that: this plan of action took me to something that I didn't even see coming that's extremely cool and lucrative for me. I have the opportunity because of that action to become a two-division champion: a Light Heavyweight and a Heavyweight Champion.

ROB:

Dude, that's awesome! That's super cool. Congratulations!

And it all comes down to deciding what you want, planning it out, and taking action.

Take a moment, and pause.

Things to think about:

- What are three things you are afraid of?

- How have those fears stopped you from success?

- What would your life be like if you overcame those fears?

Chapter 3

WHY NOT YOU?

"Inaction breeds doubt and fear. Action breeds confidence and courage. If you want to conquer fear, do not sit home and think about it. Go out and get busy."

-DALE CARNEGIE

AS SOMEONE WHO HAS TAKEN ACTION IN HIS LIFE, I've achieved a lot of success.

At one point, I leveled out in that success, and looking back I can see that one of the things that I didn't have during that time was an agent. I was booking all of my own jobs. I was actually booking nice, big jobs, and to be honest with you, I didn't look for an agent because I didn't want to get rejected by one.

During that time, I'd be watching TV with my then-wife, Nikki, and when the commercials came on, she'd always say, "Why don't you do that? Why can't you do that? You know, you do great voiceovers." We were living a comfortable life; we were doing well. I'd achieved success. I got into radio. I accomplished a lot, but I still had this belief that some things were out of my reach.

I was afraid. My fear of rejection was looming, and you know what? Nikki kept on my case, "Why don't you get an agent? When are you going to get those big jobs?"

I couldn't see it then, so I could only respond, "No, no, no."

I didn't understand it, but I was limiting my own growth.

Nikki remained supportive of my career and all the work I did to provide for our family. One night, she looked at me and said, "Rob. Why not you? Why not YOU? Why can't YOU have that top agent? Why can't YOU be the voice on all those TV commercials that you want to be on?"

She kept on my case, "It's going to be someone, Rob. Why not YOU?"

Those words were an incredible part of my life journey, and they catapulted me to the next level of success. I was sure it should be someone else, but it kept coming back to, "why not me?"

Yeah! WHY NOT ME?

So here's what I did. I sent an email to Dani's Agency, a voiceover agency who was highly recommended by my peers, and said, "Hi, I'm Rob Actis, and I'm a voiceover talent. I've done this, this and this, and here is my demo reel."

Shortly after, she sent an email back saying, "Loved your audition. Come in, let's talk."

I went in and she flat out said, "I would love to have you be part of our agency."

And then, get this, she says, "Where have you been hiding?"

I could only be honest: "Well, I was afraid you might say no, and I didn't want to feel rejected if by chance you didn't want to sign me."

She looked at me like I had three heads and said, "Do you know how much work I could have booked you for? *Do you?*"

Thank you, Nikki, for saying those words I so needed to hear: "Why not you?"

The same goes for you. As you go through life and see those wonderful things that are happening around you, just ask yourself, "Why not me?"

- Why not YOU?

- Why can't YOU be the next top model?

- Why can't YOU be the supervisor at work?

- Why can't YOU be the top sales person?

- Why can't YOU be the best plumber in the country?

- Why can't YOU be a free-diver?

- Why can't YOU be an MMA World Champion?

- Why can't YOU be a successful business coach?

- Why can't YOU be an IT analyst?

- Why can't YOU open a franchise?

- Why can't YOU declutter your entire life and become a superhero at the top of your game?

- Why can't YOU be a Hollywood director?

- Why can't YOU be an internationally known boudoir photographer?

- Why can't YOU be a top LinkedIn expert?

- Why can't YOU turn a simple idea into a multi-million-dollar company?

- Why can't YOU be the pioneer of the CBD revolution?

- Why can't YOU be a YouTube expert?

- Why can't YOU own a custom hot rod shop?

- Why can't YOU be a fitness coach for elite athletes?

- Why can't YOU be radio personality?

- Why can't YOU be a voice for your generation?

- Why can't YOU be a Top Gun pilot?

- Why can't YOU inspire millions to wake up early and start their day powerfully?

- Why can't YOU self-publish forty-four books?

- Why can't YOU be a Hollywood makeup artist?

- Why can't YOU be a Reiki master?

- Why can't YOU be an insurance agent?

- Why can't YOU be an event planner?

- Why can't YOU be awarded a star on the Hollywood Walk of Fame?

- Why can't YOU teach people about the magic of money and abundance?

- Why can't YOU be a book editor for bestselling authors?

- Why can't YOU be a nurse?

- Why can't YOU be a fire chief?

- Why can't YOU be an industry leader and inspire millions to achieve success? Why can't YOU be a top-tier voice actor agent?

- Why can't YOU be an author?

- Why can't YOU be a business banker?

- Why can't YOU be anything your heart desires?

The answer to each of the above is: you can!

You deserve it. Don't hold yourself back. You deserve to be great. You *are* great. If you're taking action, you are moving forward, and if you're moving forward, you deserve what's in front of you.

Don't be the person that stops you from your own success.

I've worked with some very talented people as a voice actor. Some of my professional contacts have become good friends—like director and producer Bruce Caulk—and those relationships are gold to me. Bruce grew up in the film business. He, too, has had his share of challenges, but by following his dreams and putting the Law of Action into place, he jumped into being an artist from early on and has been making films ever since. The feature film he is working on now is coming out the year of this writing; it's called *Con Man* and is being released by Sony.

I've always enjoyed working with Bruce. He's a great storyteller, so I've asked him to talk about his life and how the Law of Action applies to him.

We worked together on some pretty cool commercials, Rob. You did a good job adding your voice to all the commercials that we shot on 35mm film. I always fought to have the highest quality for even the regional hamburger spots. We made really kick-ass ones. And I brought you in 'cause you had a unique, friendly voice. We have been friends for so many years, and it's nice to keep that relationship going; means a lot to me. It started by being professionals together, when your craft and my craft got together. If you find talented people, there's no reason not to keep re-working with them, even if you don't see them for a decade.

As for my story, early on, just out of film school, I decided I wanted to be a writer/director. I love all aspects of filmmaking. I love cinematography, putting it all together, the story, the scripts, the sound and editing, it's a big puzzle. I've always loved puzzles. Then I moved to San Diego, where I got married and raised a family. I wanted to be a good dad; I would never trade my family life for more time in Hollywood, so I worked on commercials and documentaries. As the boys grew up, I wanted to get out of the corporate video commercial world and into feature films. Even though I made some plans about that, I kept doing the same smaller type of videos. There was nothing wrong with them, but I knew that my career bucket should be bigger, and my talents could go into mainstream Hollywood and compete for Oscars.

There was also a fear that I might fail. There was a mental story that I would run in my head since I grew up around such success as a kid—my stepdad was an agent and his clients were Oscar-winning actors—that I wouldn't be able to shine at that level.

For many years, I kept playing small and doing $10,000 and $100,000 corporate videos, and I never pushed myself. Deep down, I knew I could be an A-list director, but I held myself back. I got close to Hollywood, but there was a certain amount of fear and lack of trust. Yeah, I needed to be there for my kids and be a good dad, but maybe that was an excuse to not have to jump into the water. Eventually, I got the opportunity and seized the moment, but I lost about a decade by just talking about it and telling the story about my growing up in the biz versus actually getting out there and shooting movies. I thought that by association, I would be seen as a good director who could do big movies, but I never really tackled it. I never jumped in.

There's a nebulous sort of question about being an artist, and you really just gotta do it and see if people like it, and if you like it and feel good about it.

I'm just getting started now. I look back and say, "If you had just acted..." I could have avoided wasting so much time. Whether you win or lose is not the point. We hold ourselves back at times. Once you jump in, you never regret it. I could have jumped in sooner and at least tested what I could do, but it's part of the journey; it's in God's hands and his timeline. I'm here now and am finally committing to excellence as a director and writer.

Bruce spent a decade planning, ten full years just talking about his dreams, but never took the final step in the Law of Action until recently.

So I asked him about *Con Man* and how the feature film was coming together.

I got the opportunity to direct my first feature film—it was called *Minkow* at the time (now *Con Man*)—and we ended up having a great cast of James Caan, Ving Rhames, Mark Hamill, Talia Shire, Justin Baldoni, Elisabeth Rohm and Armand Assante. One Golden Globe winner and two Oscar-nominated actors in my first film. It was no accident that they agreed to be cast in my first movie, because of my training as an actor, the documentary experience that landed me an EMMY Award for directing, and my childhood around Oscar-winning writers and attending movie screenings on studio lots since my youth.

I navigated the waters and really delivered a good film telling the Barry Minkow/ZZZZ Best story about the youngest guy to defraud Wall Street. It was a redemption story. I was so proud of it, but life threw me for a loop. The movie was a bit of a propaganda film, promoting Barry, because I thought he was really a redeemed person. As it turns out, he was scamming the church, shorting stocks on FBI information, and heading back to jail before we knew it.

I had to make a decision: do we release this movie, my first feature film? As a director, I wanted to release it no matter what. It was on its way to Cannes. It was an opportunity to lift my career and launch myself. But knew that what he said was not true, therefore there was a lie in the movie we made.

I had a hard decision to make. Do I let the distributors run it? Or do I stop the whole post-production phase and the distribution of the movie? I told the investors we were releasing a film that's got a lie in it. Not only that, but a major lie.

I had to ask myself, "What do I want?" And I knew I couldn't let the movie be released. I negotiated with the investor, got the rights to the film, and held up the distribution.

My plan was to shoot a brand-new third act. But Barry Minkow had played himself, and I couldn't get him because he was back in jail.

Then my plan was to raise a couple million dollars and just redo the whole movie. Re-engineer it. But I found out it wasn't that easy, and though I spent a year trying to fundraise, we couldn't do it. I'd held up the movie, and I couldn't get the money to do it.

I kept planning different scenarios with different budgets on how to finish my movie, have integrity, and make a more interesting story. Because the story now is redemption gone wrong. Which is a really interesting theme. Right? Rise, fall, rise, fall. You don't hear that very often.

We did find money, as fate would have it, to redo the film in a new way. It still captures the story, but the style is better by far. It has interviews with people who were really in Barry's life. It became a profoundly powerful way to finish it.

I made the choice to get the money, and we reshot and re-edited it. I got a full orchestra from Prague and found a great composer to re-score the movie. It took four years or so to do this, and now it's a movie I can be proud of. It's still my first feature, but it's a better movie by far. And it tells the truth now, as told by those around him. Everyone who has seen both versions from the beginning has said, "Wow. This is a much more intense, interesting movie." Then Sony picked it up, which was better than what we'd had before. It's being released on March 6 (of 2018), and I'm going to be moving up as a feature director now. I also came in to do some writing on it, and worked as a co-producer as well.

There was a lot of risk, and the end result didn't happen quickly. But it ended up playing out as well as it possibly could have. I've made a high-quality and interesting film. I stuck to my guns and it paid off, because I have a studio picking up my first movie. Which is, of course, a good thing. I Decided I was going to do it, I followed the Plan, and I kept taking Action. I could not be happier with the result.

It isn't always immediate, but you can get there. All you have to do is go for it.

"Why not you?"

Every time you see something you want, go after it! You want a Lamborghini?

Well, why not you?

Take the steps that are necessary to go get that Lamborghini, if that's what you want.

What do you want in your life? What comes to mind?

I want to find a partner, no, wait, I want to find an _incredible_ partner!

I want to get married and live happily ever after!

Well, WHY NOT YOU? Why can't you have that?

I can tell you with absolute certainty that the Law of Action will take you anywhere you want to go, and how you use—or *don't* use—it dictates where your life is today.

If your life is not so great, look back on the actions that you've taken or not taken. The great part is that it's all about you, right now, today, right this minute; you can take action and change the course of your life.

You deserve it. You deserve to have an extraordinary life.

Decide, Plan, Act.

One thing I hope you took from Bruce's story is how he's now working his dream job as a director, producer and writer. It wasn't easy to get there, but he took the steps needed to make it happen.

The same can happen for you; let's take a look now at applying the Law of Action to your career.

Using the Law of Action for Getting Your Dream Job

- **Decide** you are ready to receive the job offer of your dreams. Imagine what it feels like to have it. Really FEEL that excitement and know it's time to move into that job.

- **Plan** to accept that job by asking yourself, "What tangible things need to happen?" Listen to your inner guidance, thoughts and feelings. Take mental notes, then turn those into physical notes you can review. Be unrealistic and ambitious! You are about to have your dream job!

- **Act.** This may mean applying for a specific job or sending an amazing résumé to places you want to work for. Maybe it means making phone calls or putting word out to friends or social contacts. Do it.

I knew I wanted to be in radio when I was really little, and I kept at it until it happened. Asking for what I wanted was a huge part of that, as was connecting with the right people who would be able to open doors for me.

I'll never forget the first time I was able to actually crack the mic open and talk on the air on B100. It was during the late '80s, on Christmas Day. Bobby Rich was my boss and a very kind mentor, and he scheduled me to come in on Christmas Day and do very basic talking between Christmas songs live on the air. It was a Christmas miracle! Keep in mind, this was a *huge* deal for me, a dream come true. I'd been working my way up to this moment my whole life, previously I'd only played pre-recorded tracks from DJ's but this was me, live.

Best Christmas ever! I was all over it. Bobby told me to not go overboard, to just stick with the basics. I did what he asked, and it was going well. Then the hotline rang—the radio version of the Bat phone; when someone calls that number, it's important. It was Bobby. He told me he was listening and gave me a huge compliment for doing what I was asked. He told me that that jocks get more chances when they follow the rules. He congratulated me on following the rules. Yay, me!

Because I was following the rules and had proven myself to him, and he told me I could do the weather and top-of-the-hour ID. He told me to just be a little more Rob. He continued to trust me and give me more responsibilities and freedom in the following months.

He allowed me to do the local live DJ cut-ins on a National Countdown show, and then I became the host of the B100 Saturday Night Dance Party I hosted.

I have so much gratitude for Bobby Rich. He saw my passion for radio and let me in the door. He has spent his entire career in broadcasting and loves what he does. Of course, he learned some stuff along the way too. Here's some wisdom that he shared:

> For me, a "big idea" includes any and every element that contributes to total success. There must be a perceived desire for the product. Creating a radio station that just plays music you like does NOT guarantee a ratings magnet.
>
> My first "built from scratch" station format was 100.7fm in San Diego, CA. The technical work was in place, and the station was airing a failing background music format. There would be no hold-over audience to be concerned about.
>
> Multi-million-dollar businesses won't make sweeping changes without a business plan and someone with a track record to execute it. Here's where being patient helped me immensely; I had been employed by the company for eight months before making my presentation.
>
> They got to know me, along with my ideas, approaches and results. I shared my gut instincts about the market's needs and used those points throughout the initial interviews. Once they were convinced that I was their choice, I had a strong position from which to negotiate. I demanded complete control over all decisions that would affect the on-air product.
>
> There was a distinct plan for the DJ personalities: they would sound warm, have great energy and be "ageless" (a listener would not know how old they were, but they would definitely sound like young adults). I hired great people and coached them to be knowledgeable about what the format required them to do and not do. Then I encouraged them to make their own good choices when they saw the opportunity to improve the flow of the station.

Our top priority in content was the community. They were even instructed to say "San Diego" whenever it fit. At this time, nearly all stations called themselves by their legal name (call letters), which were assigned by the Federal Communications Commission (FCC). Ours were KFMB-fm (KFMB-am and KFMB-tv were also part of the family.) A call letter change could eliminate confusion and long-held images for the "other" KFMB products, but ownership denied my request. The challenge was to make the product something that sounded different than KFMB-fm. My solution was to call it B100 (the dial position was 100.7, but this was before digital radio dials). FCC requirements of stating the legal name once an hour were met by adding a pause and an emphasis: "K—fm. B—fm. San Diego's FM at 100.7 is B100." It was completely legal and sounded unlike any other station.

Fighting to keep control of the "little things," I stayed out of what was less important but kept my focus and priorities on everything that could affect the sound and image of the product. I won nearly every battle internally. And, thanks to the amazing team assembled and all those "little things," we became the first contemporary FM station in the country to reach number one ratings status.

B100 became a leader station being copied and imitated by hundreds of stations.

Believe in yourself. Adopt a solid level of confidence. Fight for what you know. Don't stand down from accepting anything that you know is just "good enough." One of these things is not like the other: sometimes "good enough" has to be good enough, and not standing down can harm your initial plan unnecessarily. Maturity plays into this more than we ever know—or admit—in our younger years.

Around 1990, in Seattle, I made many mistakes. First by letting ego and passion allow me to accept a job that was not offered because I was the best candidate, but because the people who were trying to hire me wanted me out of San Diego so that I would not be competing with one of their other stations. KNOW YOUR STRENGTHS (and weaknesses). Mostly the same scenario, but this time with hands tied and eyes shut to reality, I was hired to be the savior of a station based on my track record. I did not seek out this situation; they came after me. The money and position were far beyond anything I had previously done. Consultants, informers, unhappy employees, et al, got the ear of top management, and ultimately I was fired. (Not before I was put through an attempt to humiliate and berate my industry image, though...) Fortunately, I negotiated my own exit with favorable monetary outcome.

It's embarrassing to admit, but the very same scenario played out at my next job. Again, I didn't trust my gut feelings and bowed to the prestigious position and big bucks offered. I was fired after four months, leading to nearly a year of unemployment. My next move was a bad example of believing your heart and ignoring your head. I invested all of my savings to buy an equity position in yet another radio station. Eleven months later, they were bankrupt, and I lost everything. Biggest learning moment: ASK THE RIGHT QUESTIONS. If you don't know them, find someone who can tell you. In retrospect, I realize I always did my best work when I started slow and created a solution to an existing problem with a doable business plan. Right on, Bobby; you've gotta decide that your dream is worth fighting for, plan to not let anyone stand in your way, and take action by moving steadily forward.

Debunking the Myth of Overnight Success

There's no such thing as overnight success. Successful people have taken action steps to get where they are. Everybody has had their own journey. It's never too early or too late to begin.

I recently met an amazing millennial, Alison Lea Sher. She is still young but has had an amazing life journey already. She's writing a book right now, too. I asked her if I could interview her for this book, and she was all in. What she said inspired me even more. Rob:

Thanks so much, Alison, for taking the time to share your story with me. I'm fascinated with millennials, especially the way they think and interact in today's world. You seem to be someone who can really share their perspective. Would you please tell me a bit about yourself?

ALISON:

Okay. Cool. I'm the founder and CEO of Millennial Inc. I'm also the author of an upcoming book called *The Millennial's Guide to Changing the World*. That's going to be out in May, 2018, under the publishing house, Skyhorse Publishing.

I'm a writer, editor, speaker, and consultant. I have a ten-year background in publishing and journalism. To write my book, I went around the country, living in an RV for a year. I interviewed over 200 members of my generation for the field research to write my book and start my consulting company. I've been studying our current system for over five years. I wanted to figure out how it all works, the nuts and bolts in every single sector of society, how the problems my generation are inheriting evolved into being and the solutions people from all generations are inventing to save humanity (as dramatic as that sounds). I think a huge component to all of this involves millennials stepping up to our potential to become more active in the world so we can incorporate our values and ideas into this social structure—because they are the values and inspiration that are needed to transform the world.

ROB:

Wow, that's amazing, Alison. So your book is geared toward millennials who maybe aren't quite sure how to navigate the current world?

ALISON:

Yes. A lot of people would say that this giant generation is underperforming. That they are suffering from a sort of arrested development. I wanted to study that, mainly because I was suffering from it. My book is what you call an ethnographic study—a study of a culture made by the people inside of it. One of my key hypotheses revolves around the concept of intersectionality and how we increase our consciousness of cause and effect. Humanity has to unite over some common goals and get over our egos while still being ourselves. Millennials need to choose and pursue a life purpose—for our own survival and for own emotional development. I don't have a singular prescription for anyone, though my book does give people a roadmap to go about creating their lives in an informed way. It's filled with all the lessons I learned the hard way, while in my twenties. This whole process has been character-building. It's important to finish things. If nothing else, I've grown tremendously throughout this project.

ROB:

Nice. I like it. I like it. So, the first question is...with the Law of Action in mind, what great accomplishment have you achieved after you made the decision to actually do it, planned how to do it, then taken action?

ALISON:

Ah. The most notable and biggest accomplishment is getting this book deal. I don't have a very large following yet, so it was really kind of miraculous. I think it was a testament to my concept that I was offered a professional publishing deal for this book, when the market is so competitive.

You know, it's funny because I spent a lot of my early twenties being really indecisive about what I wanted to do with my life. My huge ego was hung up on figuring out the most powerful thing I could possibly do to save the planet—as if that task was my sole responsibility. I put too much pressure on myself. It made everything way too painful, and it was kind of delusional. I was so afraid of what would happen if I failed.

In the end, I just had to throw my cards down on something, and I chose this. From thinking about the concept, to doing all this research on the road and interviewing all of these people...it was a significant time investment. Then we also had a crowdfunding campaign that raised over $23,000. So much money and time have gone into this book...wow, thinking about it now...there was getting an agent, sending out the book proposal just to get rejected by hundreds of publishing houses. When I finally got a deal, I was like, "Whoa! I can really make something happen." But by that time I had also learned how to release my attachments to the outcome, so I could stay sane while going about this project.

ROB:

Thank you for acknowledging the work it takes. It is a lot of work when we take action. I like to say it's not easy, but it's simple: you just keep taking action. Keep moving.

ALISON:

It's especially hard the first time you go out and do something like that. I think that's what is keeping so many millennials stuck at the starting gate. It's a vulnerable thing to make yourself visible in the world, because people are mean and most won't care about you until you give them a reason to. You need self-esteem to be able put a stake down and be like, "This is my offering to the planet, and it matters." I would like to see more millennials become stakeholders of our future. I think that's something the world needs.

ROB:

You are a massive action taker. I admire that. Do you feel that is a common trait in millennials?

ALISON:

Well, what I've seen with a lot of my peers is they want it to be easy. People who are New Age-y think this whole Law of Attraction idea is their saving grace, like everything they want will just plop into their lap, but that's not really how things manifest. That may be the way things manifested during our childhood. But in the real world, you have to make moves. In my twenties, I came up with a long list of shit that doesn't work. But in doing so I figured a lot out because I went for it, and I believe that it's all been perfect. Now, I have so much more confidence, but I had to fail first. I'm going to see what happens and bring this idea to fruition. Regardless of what happens, I know I will be able to put myself out there again. It gets easier and easier every time that I do it. Someone once told me that if you have ideas, you'll always be fine in this world. But maybe it's truer that you'll always be fine if you have ideas and actually take action.

ROB:

Nice. I like that. So, were you stuck at any time? What were the hardest parts of your process?

ALISON:

Well, I'll tell you this. I've worked with many people along the way, and I have learned a lot about who I am, what I need, and how to be honest with myself about how things are going. I was so afraid to spearhead this project alone because of my own neuroses that I ended up compromising my goals to meet other's ideals, just to keep from facing that fear. It just created a lot of unresolvable conflict in my life. I got pretty stuck and self-sacrificial during parts of this, but I also got through it. I made the decision to believe in myself.

Luckily, I had this amazing agent who is very close to me in my life now. When I knew I had to leave behind my creative partner and the brand we had built, my agent told me that she would still represent me as I built myself back up. I was given an amazing opportunity that was kind of like a turning point. I couldn't shake this idea. I had already invested so much, and I had to pull myself up by my bootstraps and find the self-worth to be like, *You know what, my idea rocks.* Like, this idea is amazing. I'm talented. And this is what I've wanted to achieve my whole life. It's not over yet.

ROB:

You overcame fears and owned your idea, right?

ALISON:

I had to get very real with myself and analyze my intentions for doing this. I kind of had a rebirth in the process. I suffered from youthful narcissism or something, thinking that this book's success would solve my problems and I'd be a hero and prove everyone who told me I couldn't make it wrong. Really, the world doesn't need that. It just needs me to be good to the people around me, and it's hard to do that when you're consumed by yourself.

I made everything too serious, when creating things can be fun. If I come from a space where I'm in alignment, where I'm not willing to pull any weird power plays to get what I want from anyone else, usually things work out. I have a lot less emotional attachment to my work and have found that I can produce a lot more—and quickly—when I'm emotionally balanced about what I'm doing. I've asked myself many times, "Why am I writing this book?" And my final answer is that I'm writing this book because I love to write books.

This is not going to be my last, but rather just my first. I'm going to finish it, not because my ego's attached to becoming influential and famous to validate the purpose of my existence, but because not giving up throughout it all has really helped me to build some character. I think there's a lot of character that's built when we see things to completion, regardless of the obstacles that come up. When you have an idea that you can't shake, just do it. You'll be a different person than when you started if you get it done.

ROB:

I love it, and I agree with you completely on that. Can you think of a project or something in your life that you decided you wanted and you planned for it but never actually finished it?

ALISON:

Well, I learned how important it is to focus on the planning stage, because without it, things are a lot harder to get done. I started this project without the essential business documents and agreements everyone needs to enter a partnership with informed consent. You know when you're young and full of ideas and excitement and don't think about making win-win agreements? That's what I did. Things got complicated quite quickly, and I went through a lot of turmoil trying to make it work. It cost me a lot of time and money, caused me to lose a relationship, and threatened my ability to bring my dreams into fruition. I was almost crushed by the conflict.

I take responsibility for that. I take responsibility for my fear and desperation and lack of self-worth that made me ignore all the signs that it wasn't a good fit. I was also just young, wanting to be an adult, without knowing an adult way to go about making these kinds of deals. I forgive myself for it.

I've had to learn that whatever I create is a product of my own psyche. I had to do a lot psycho-emotional work after the partnership disbanded, to clear out those issues so the thing that I would create in the aftermath could actually come from an aligned place. So I could walk my talk. So the book might actually benefit someone.

ROB:

That's amazing ownership of yourself, Alison. You are such an inspiration! Speaking with you now, I'd never think you had self-worth issues.

ALISON:

Now I'm in a solid space. When this book comes out, I'll be proud of it and proud of who I am. I will be able to go around and speak about it, because I don't care as much what people think of me anymore. I believe that we're here to be creators. We're here to do what we can to minimize the suffering of others and bring joy to the world in the process. My intuition has always told me that this brilliant book project is how I'm supposed to do it. And I've decided to be humble and listen, roll the dice, and see what happens. It requires true confidence.

ROB:

Yes. Absolutely. Thank you for sharing such a beautiful part of yourself, and your story. You are amazing and unique and seem to be quite a leader among millennials. You have given me some great insight, and I look forward to reading your book!

ALISON:

Thank you so much for interviewing me. Let's inspire some people to take action!

How about that?

We have so many tools to create the life we want. I invite you to stop for a moment and look at *your* life.

Instead of looking at other people's lives and wishing and hoping you could be them, look at YOU. What are the things that are holding you back?

Why are you looking at your own life and thinking, "Well, I can do that," but then you aren't actually doing it yet?

"Why not YOU?"

Look at all those "Why not you?" questions we talked about previously and re-evaluate. Take a moment, and pause. You. Yes, you. Why not you?

The bridge between where you are and what you desire is...yep, you guessed it...

Decide, Plan, Act.

You deserve to be great. YOU deserve to have success. YOU DESERVE a happily ever after. Are you willing to do what it takes?

Because the Law of Action is what it takes.

We've already talked about taking massive, immediate action, and it's go, go, go. Decide, Plan, Act. Decide, Plan, Act.

Note that it isn't supposed to be painful the whole time. If it is, pause and reflect. Think about what you're doing and, more importantly, *why*.

It's really important to enjoy your life! I mean, that IS the whole point! Do what you love, and love what you do. Ask yourself, "Am I having fun?"

Check in on a regular basis. When you're on your right path, it's fun. It may not always be easy or simple, but it's fun, because you know you're on the ride that you want to be on.

If you want to be on the kiddie ride, then be on the kiddie ride, and have that be your ride, and enjoy that kiddie ride. If you want to be on the merry-go-round, be on the merry-ground. If you want to be on the loop-de-loop Skycoaster that's 500 feet in the air and suddenly drops, and you get an adrenaline rush just from riding it, do that.

The Law of Action asks you to be honest with yourself about what is best for you.

Decide, Plan, Act.

Every day, ask yourself, "Am I having fun?" Every day, plan something to have fun. Decide, Plan, Act to have fun.

You might play some music and dance to a favorite song. I really enjoy listening to lots of different kinds of music, and I love to dance. I also love karaoke! What do you love to do?

When you are obeying the Law of Action, you should be having fun! Face challenges head on, and work through them.

It's always a balance, remember?

Work, play, rest.

In the past, I have felt guilty when I played. I worked really, *really* hard, and I worked all the time. Then I Decided, Planned, and Acted on balancing it out.

What I've discovered is that when I take time off to play and rest, I come back to my work refreshed and energized. It took me a long time to figure that out.

See? I'm still human.

What if you've forgotten how to play? Prioritize finding your joy, right now.

Using the Law of Action for Finding Your Joy

- **Decide** you deserve to have fun and joy in your life. Feel that laughter and easy smile that you had when you were a kid. Kids are great at playing! Think about what simple things you enjoy now.

- **Plan** to spend one minute feeling joy every day, then increase it to five minutes, then an hour, then...three hours! You might have to actually SCHEDULE time to play until you get good at it. Put it on your calendar and devote time to it. Exercising your laughter muscles is just as important as working out, so give it that much priority.

- **Act** on creating your joy! Keep a humorous book by the toilet. Make a YouTube playlist of videos that make you smile, and watch one every day. Spend time with your kids or pets.

Play. Play. Play!

Whether you're into karaoke, kayaking, dancing, scrapbooking, horseback riding, playing sports, or whatever your heart desires—you have to have fun. The Law of Action requires the balance of...

Work, play, rest.

I'll talk a lot about the importance of rest and mindfulness later in the book. Just remember for now that it's so important to take breaks. You know, stop and smell the roses. Enjoy your life.

One of the things that I really enjoy doing is going to TopGolf; there is one just a few minutes from my house in Gilbert, Arizona. Now, people who know me will be really surprised that I am talking about golf, since I am not really one of those sports-centered guys. I am normally a very competitive person, but when I go to TopGolf, I do not have much concern of my score. The more I've practiced driving the ball, the better I have gotten, and I must say: hitting a golf ball with a driver can be a very Zen-like experience.

I do NOT go to TopGolf because I am an avid golfer; I go because it is fun. I enjoy the atmosphere. Since I don't have a physical office, TopGolf has become my place to focus and work while indulging my love of the outdoors and enjoying the beautiful scenery. I wrote the majority of this book while sitting in my favorite bay and, when I got frustrated, I could stand up, hit a few balls, let the frustration go, and get back to work.

They also have music and great food, which becomes more of a party atmosphere at night, but I tend to go during the day when there are a lot of fellow entrepreneurs working also. It is a very relaxed environment, and I have been fortunate to have some pretty cool conversations with high-profile entrepreneurs. I love getting to know people; there is something really special about hearing people's stories.

A couple weeks ago, I was there, and I noticed two guys wearing Costa Vida shirts. That happens to be one of my favorite places to eat, so I struck up a conversation with them. It turned out they were brothers and also the owners of a bunch of Costa Vida franchises in Arizona.

I asked if I could interview them for my book because I was including stories about successful entrepreneurs and was a huge fan of their restaurant. They agreed, and I spoke with Dano, one of the two brothers I met. Their life story started out like many others before it took a turn down the rocky entrepreneurial road. Dano:

I was born in Miami, then grew up in Utah. Brad and I played sports all kinds growing up. That was our childhood; until the sun went down and our parents called us in, we played outside with our friends all day.

We both served LDS (Latter-Day Saints) missions, came back, got married within a year or so, then went to college.

I'd known for a long time that I wanted to run a business, so I started looking at business opportunities. Our dad was an entrepreneur who worked with the state, placing kids in homes for foster care. We saw the lifestyle that it afforded him. More than anything, that lifestyle was the appeal, so I knew I wanted to own or run a business.

After exploring a few options, I was led to Costa Vida. It was a brand-new restaurant, a franchise with two locations in Utah. Brad and I loved the place, so we talked about getting involved. Mind you, we had zero restaurant experience.

We knew business from our dad, though, so we talked with him about the idea, and he said he'd be willing to get involved. Then we reached out to Costa Vida. They were desperate for franchisees and needed good people.

Because I had zero restaurant experience, I quit my job and worked at their corporate location for eight bucks an hour so I could learn the ins and outs. I worked every position: cook, dishwasher, cashier... everything.

Within a few months, I had worked my way up and become the general manager, which enabled me to learn every aspect of what it takes to run that restaurant. We ended up moving to Arizona and taking over an existing location in Mesa, the only one outside of Utah at the time. That third location of Costa Vida had been built in 2005 and was not doing very well. We bought it in March of 2007. When we visited before we moved to Arizona, we were able to see what needed to be done to get that location in the black.

That restaurant was our life. We worked 90-hour weeks and turned the store around fast. It was a huge blessing, but also really scary. The necessary changes we made disrupted the culture, and we had to let over ten people go. Our intention wasn't to come in and clean house, but we had to let a lot of people go. Then a lot of people we wanted to keep left with them because we had fired their friends. It was a very stressful time. We lost a lot of weight. My first night going to bed, I cried myself to sleep and thought, "What have we gotten ourselves into?"

After months and months of just grinding away and sticking to it, things worked out, and in 2009 we opened our second location in Queen Creek. The Goodyear location opened in 2011 but only lasted a year and a half. Then the Tempe Costa Vida opened in 2013, followed by the Gilbert location in 2016.

Once there were more restaurants than the two of us, we had to start hiring managers so that we could step out of the restaurants and actually work on the business rather than work in the business. Rob:

Wow. What a great success story. You *decided* you wanted to get a restaurant. You liked the concept. You *planned* for it. You went in and worked. Then you took *action* and bought it. Now, because you did that and you worked your butts off, you have the success of multiple restaurants. So, you guys are the only owners of the Costa Vida restaurants in Arizona?

DANO:

As of now, yes, but the territory is open, so there could be others. Some have tried and closed. When we came down to Arizona, we were able to get the business into the black because of what we had learned in Utah. We've grown ever since. There are now four locations in the Phoenix Valley: Tempe, Queen Creek, Gilbert, and Mesa.

ROB:

Congratulations! You worked so hard to get there, pushing through and sticking with it even when it was a huge challenge. Have you always been this successful? So many people would have given up...

DANO:

In a lot of ways, yes, but I had to overcome failure from when I was about thirteen. I had tried out for the Olympic Development Program, a soccer team, at the earliest stage of eligibility. I made the preliminary team, which had a larger pool of players that they were trimming down to create the team. Long story short, after a few weeks of traveling, I was handed a pink slip at the end of practice. I didn't know what it was, so I just took it and tossed it in the car with my stuff.

I gave it to my mom, and she asked me if I knew what it was. I said, "No, they didn't say anything to me." I just figured it was something about a practice or game. She read it and told me I had been cut from the team.

Not only was it devastating, it was also a little bit embarrassing because they didn't even tell me. I was very hurt and upset about it.

Even though I continued to play soccer for multiple teams over the years growing up, I didn't feel like I was worthy to try out again for that Olympic-level team. When I reached the final year of eligibility for it, at seventeen or eighteen, I did try out, and I made the team.

I even made it to regionals and the All-Star team, and got recruited to play at Coastal Carolina back east, a Division 1 school. But I didn't get a scholarship. They hadn't seen me in the previous years, so I missed out because of my fear to go and try out again, even though I knew I wanted it. I had *decided* and *planned* on playing soccer in college, but I just never went and took the *action* of trying out again because I was afraid I wouldn't make it.

ROB:

So, in essence, your fear of not making it became your reality. What did you do in those four years that helped you break through that fear to where you went back in and took action?

DANO:

I just continued to work hard, honestly. I was playing on a club team, a high school team, and an indoor team. I continued to work at the craft. I must have been convinced from that young age and earlier experience that I wasn't good enough. It kept me from going and putting myself at risk of suffering embarrassment.

ROB:

So that possibly stopped you from even going to the Olympics?

DANO:

It's possible. I don't want to go that far and say, "Oh I would have made Nationals." But yeah, sure, it is a possibility. The fact that I didn't try out again, and let so much time go between the first cut and my last opportunity...you never know how that might have gone, but it definitely made my wheels turn on what else could have been possible. It also gave me strength to not give up, to keep at whatever I do and see it through.

When I began to interview people for this book, I was impressed by how many people have overcome really tough challenges. Life is such a gift, and we get to experience all of it. The hard stuff, the fun stuff, and the huge breakthroughs.

It's all part of this beautiful life. Don't miss it!

Take time out, and breathe. Look at the beautiful colors of the flowers. I know that might sound trite and silly, but seriously, do that. Stop for a moment. Take your shoes off and walk in the grass. Get grounded with this amazing planet Earth. Connect with Mother Nature.

You deserve to feel good. You deserve to get good rest, and most of all you deserve to enjoy your life!

You are worthy!

Don't believe the story that you aren't worthy. It will stop everything you want to do. Trust me; I have walked that path and busted up the lie of "I'm not worthy."

Since that day, my life has taken a major turn for the better.

Take a moment, and pause.

Things to think about:

- Who do you look up to?

- Thinking of your role models, which one do you want to be most like?

- What is stopping you, and how can you use the Law of Action to move toward your dreams?

Chapter 4

THE "I'M NOT WORTHY" LIE

"Action is the real measure of intelligence."

-NAPOLEON HILL

Your time is limited, so don't waste it living someone else's life. Don't be trapped by dogma - which is living with the results of other people's thinking. Don't let the noise of others' opinions drown out your own inner voice. And most important, have the courage to follow your heart and intuition.

-STEVE JOBS

WE ALL HAVE DOUBTS. UNFORTUNATELY, OUR DOUBTS CAN stop us from taking action. People look at me sometimes and say, "Wow, you've got it all going on—you're super successful, you do all these TV commercials and radio commercials and big projects."

I say, "You know what, let me tell you a story."

I followed the Law of Action to get where I am today.

I Decided, I Planned, and I Acted, and have become an accomplished voice actor.

This is what my days look like: I get an audition from my agent, then go into my recording booth in my studio, record the audio, edit it, and send off the audition.

Whether it was a little job or a big job, it was the same process.

Sometimes I'd get auditions and I'd call my agent, Anthony, and ask, "Why'd you send me this?" Because to me, it just did not feel like it was a job suited for me.

He'd tell me, "Look, I don't send you anything that you're not ready for. I don't send you anything that you're not perfect for. You're already 98 percent of the way there, we just have to see if they pick you. You already have the ability to do it."

But I still had doubts.

Once in a while, an audition comes in that just makes me feel unworthy. An example of that was an audition that was sent to me a couple years ago. It was for a high-profile client—a national campaign for Bayer Aspirin.

You've probably heard of Bayer Aspirin, right?

It was for a fifteen-second TV spot.

I looked at the description of the voice, the tone, and how it would be used.

When I saw how big of a campaign it was going to be, the little voice in my head said, "You know, you can't do this. You're not worthy. You're not going to be able to do this."

So I didn't.

I was terrified. Paralyzed by fear. And I felt really dumb.

After some time, I went back and looked at the email again. I stared at it and couldn't bring myself to record the audition. I spent a LOT of time looking at that email and still didn't do it.

I can't recall what clicked, but after so much time not taking action, and letting it bug me, I said, "You know what...I'm going to try it."

I went into my booth and voiced the audition. When I listened to the recording, I told myself, "Nah, they're not going to like me. There's no way I'll get this."

That "I'm not worthy" monster came into my brain.

Then something interesting happened. I stepped back and looked deep into myself.

I asked myself, "Rob, what is going on here?" (No, I didn't answer. Okay, maybe I did...)

I had already done four auditions that day. They weren't giant jobs like this one, but they were big jobs, and there had been no hesitation whatsoever.

On this one, my brain was persistent: "You can't be this successful."

But what did that mean? The difference between the other auditions I had already easily completed and this big one was one simple thing: perception.

It really was no different than the others; it only seemed bigger and scarier because I let my mind assign a different value to it. I thought about Wayne Gretzky's quote: "You miss 100% of the shots you don't take."

What if a pro hockey player decided not to take a shot because the goalie he was facing was really skilled and he might get blocked, or he was scared of the crazy monster decal on the goalie's mask? That just wouldn't happen, right? Because they're *professionals*. And so am I. So are you, in whatever work you do.

In those moments of indecision, I said to myself, "Okay. Get centered."

Then I sat down and meditated. I got really peaceful and calm with myself, and very mindful of what was really going on.

I noticed how I was feeling unworthy.

Ultimately, I was afraid I wasn't going to get the job. The conversation with myself was interesting.

I audition for other jobs every day, and I don't get all of them. You get some, and you don't get others. That's just part of the business.

In fact, it can take dozen of auditions for the average voice actor in this stage of the game to book a job. Sometimes more, sometimes less. But the fact is, no one books every job. As in every industry, no one lands every position they apply or interview for.

Every day I get rejected, so why was this one so challenging? Even the meditation didn't get me there, so I gave up.

I called my agent, Anthony, and said, "I'm not going to do this."

He said, "If you don't want to do it, okay...thanks. I appreciate you letting me know." He didn't question me, but then he said, "Someone's going to get the job, but now there's no chance it'll be you." One thing about Anthony is that he is very no-nonsense and does not pull punches, which I respect about him.

Wow. I thought to myself, "I basically just said to him that I was not worthy and too afraid to audition." Even though I knew I was a professional at the top of my game, my fear was winning because I was too scared to even try.

I had just decided my own fate to be...not getting the job. That decision was based on *fear* of not getting the job, and I had turned it into inaction, which *guaranteed* me the end result of not getting the job.

The fear became a reality. I literally had no chance, because I was too afraid to put myself out there. My mind replayed Wayne Gretzky's quote:

"You miss 100% of the shots you don't take."

Something clicked again.

I sat down, read the script one more time, and made the decision to go into the booth. I decided to record it one time, and whatever came of that fifteen seconds was going to be my audition. I wasn't going to second guess myself.

I took the shot.

After sending the audition to my agent, the feeling was unreal!

It was like I actually got the job. I felt such a sense of accomplishment, and I thought to myself, "That was huge, because I actually worked through 'I'm not worthy' and 'Why not me?' all in that same day."

In the voiceover industry, we audition, and we audition, and we audition. If we aren't chosen and hired, we never hear back.

It's just how it is.

So once I submitted the audition, I completely forgot about it. As usual, I immersed myself in life, work, doing lots of auditions.

After a few days had passed, Anthony called and said nonchalantly, "Hey, I just want to let you know, you booked a gig."

My response was, "That's great."

He had gone on to say, "I'll give you details soon, but you booked it. By the way, it was Bayer. The one you didn't want to do."

Wow!

It felt like a bolt of lightning struck through to my core!

I got the job. *I got the job for Bayer Aspirin.*

I got it.

Long story short, I did the session, one commercial turned into four, and then a few months later, they called me back into the studio for four more commercials.

I was very well compensated for those commercials. Every time they ran on TV, I was paid, and they were run a lot. I thought to myself, "I almost sealed my fate based on fear of unworthiness." Because of an unreasonable fear, I would have missed out on significant income from that commercial.

How many times have you missed out because you were too afraid to act? I don't ask out of judgment (I've certainly been there myself) but as a way to inspire reflection. Are you ready to say enough is enough to your inner unworthiness?

Lessons in Adversity

Adversity is one of life's biggest challenges to overcome, but when you do, new doors open. What is adversity?

It's what shows up to test you, often in the form of a difficult situation or obstacle. You can let it stop your success, or you can stare it in the face and choose to be stronger than it is.

Every obstacle I have overcome has made me stronger. Getting that Bayer Aspirin job was a catalyst for greater things.

After that, I just continued to do my auditions. Booked some, not booked some, it's all part of the process. I got an audition for a Super Bowl commercial—pretty exciting—voiced the audition, sent it off to my agent, and hoped for the best.

A few weeks later, my agent, Anthony, called to let me know that I did not have the job yet, but I was getting closer. I got a callback, which typically meant I passed the first major cut and was in a small group of four or five people who would do a second audition.

I did the callback audition, fingers crossed. With it being a Super Bowl spot, I was pumped...very, very excited. Super Bowl spots are obviously high profile. I mean, some people watch the game just for the great commercials. Those spots can really make a difference in your career.

With today's technology, I usually record auditions in my home studio, but because this was a Super Bowl spot, the client requested I do it live in one of the premier recording studios in Santa Monica. I flew into LA for the job, and it was an amazing experience.

A few big-time celebrities were in the recording studio doing their thing. I could feel the energy of all the talented actors who had done work there. There was even a row of black town cars out front with the drivers waiting for the celebrities to finish their sessions.

How cool is it that my driver was parked in the same line of cars, waiting for me?

I was soaking all of this in, and though the experience was really fun, ultimately I am a professional. When I was called in to perform, I was well-rested. I brought my A game and gave it everything I had.

I was comfortable there, and the whole process took less than thirty minutes. Everything felt great. I came out feeling high as a kite, upbeat. I just had a great session in Los Angeles at a big-time studio. I got to experience the highest of the highs. It was pretty cool crossing paths with some recognizable celebrities in the hallways, not to mention that I was the voice for a Super Bowl spot.

Why not me?!

Within a few hours of finishing the session, I was on my way back to Gilbert, Arizona. When the plane landed and I turned my phone back on, I had a text from my agent that said, "Call me."

This was not the kind of text that I usually got from my agent. When I got off the plane, I called him. What transpired next was a massive buzzkill after what I had experienced just hours ago.

He was very matter-of-fact and said he had received a call from the client. In this industry, clients rarely call back with something positive to say, so I was concerned.

Anthony asked me how the session went. I told him that it was great, they complimented me and, after a few takes, they said they had everything they needed. I thanked them and left. My first thought was that they might have made a copy change, which happens often, and needed me to fly back as the Super Bowl was fast approaching.

He told me the agency rep said, "Rob is not the voice we want, and we're not gonna pay him. We made a mistake, and we picked the wrong guy. Now we have to find somebody else to do the job, so paying Rob is not in our budget."

Anthony always has my back. He made it clear that he wasn't happy about that arrangement and worked it out so I was paid after all, even though we lost the job.

Then something changed on their end, and we found out that they would keep me on the spot after all. They came back to Anthony and made it very clear that I was the right guy. That was great news, although a bit stressful, but it all worked out.

Of course, I go out and tell all my family and friends that I'm on a Super Bowl spot. It's going to be great. I'm so excited. I'll have a Super Bowl party! This is a big deal. I told everyone what to look out for, and we're watching as the commercial runs. My voice on the Super Bowl TV commercial would be the last ten seconds of it. We all watched the commercial from beginning to end, and then the room was dead silent. Everyone was confused, and I was trying to wrap my brain around what had happened.

Not only did they not use *my* voice on those last ten seconds, they didn't use anybody's voice. I was devastated and embarrassed in front of my family and friends. I felt like I had failed, and questioned even being in the voiceover business. It wasn't easy, but I worked through it and made the decision that this was not going to determine my future. It was close, though. I almost walked away from the industry and my lifelong dream. After some inner soul searching and deep meditation, I decided if I had booked a high-profile TV session once, I could do it again.

But let me tell you, the whole thing was intense.

Fast forward a few weeks. I got a call from Anthony, and he says the dreaded, "Okay, here's the deal."

This time it was not a bad thing, though; it was a very positive thing. They did not use my voice in the Super Bowl spot, but they started using it on the TV spots after the Super Bowl. The checks started to come in for those airings. It was probably my longest-running national commercial campaign.

Talk about an emotional roller coaster.

For a debilitating major setback to happen one time in my career would have been more than enough, but I got to experience it a second time, when I auditioned and was cast for another national commercial. This time, I stayed in Phoenix and did what's called an ISDN session. That means I'm in a studio in Phoenix and they're in Los Angeles and, through the wonders of modern technology, I am able to transmit my voice to LA.

During the session, there was an open mic in the room somewhere. Someone said something less-than-complimentary about the product

I was doing the voiceover for. It wasn't me, but whoever heard it on the other end in LA assumed it was, and the producer was not happy.

They called my agent and gave him an earful about it, making it clear that I would never work for them again. I told my agent that I loved the product and, actually, not only did I use it myself but I give it often as a gift. Anthony tried to reason with them, but they didn't want to hear it.

Talk about adversity.

Once again, I was devastated. This was a big client, and now I had a possible bad reputation for something I didn't even do. I worried I would be blacklisted and wondered if the voiceover industry was trying to tell me my time was up. I took some time to meditate and got very clear that this was something that I've wanted to do since I was four years old. I made the commitment to myself that I was supposed to be in this industry, and I would focus on booking other TV spots.

Instead of giving up, I had a plan of action. I decided that I wanted to be a national voice actor. I planned for it. I worked my butt off, and I took action. Six years later, I am still the voice of that TV commercial.

When I was faced with those huge, punch-in-the-gut situations, I almost gave up. It tested my will and strength in a way I never expected. I almost left the business entirely, but I remembered that "I'm not worthy" is a lie.

Learning to accept rejection is a brutal process that challenges your identity. You can't take it personally; you have to persevere and keep taking action to do that next audition, that next interview, that next job, that next project.

That's the adversity that a voiceover actor has to go through, that we all have to go through no matter our line of work.

Not taking it personally on that Super Bowl job was probably one of the hardest times in my career. Why? I got fired from a national TV commercial after doing exactly what they were telling me to do.

But I did overcome it. I didn't take it personally. I did my job, let it go, and ended up getting the work in a different way. Looking back, I realize that I not only booked the job the first time, but then it changed agencies and production houses once or twice, and they continued to use my voice. Often, new agencies will replace the voice, but my voice kept getting picked. Talk about a roller coaster ride!

If you are on the right path, and you love what you do, don't quit. Seriously, don't quit, no matter how bad things may seem. You might just be facing adversity, and when you overcome it, the door opens to the success of your dreams.

Even the Successful Feel Unworthy

I hope this inspires you to take action, even when you feel unworthy of the result you may get. Don't preempt yourself from success; if you are up at bat, you better swing.

Remember, you are worthy.

"Why not you?"

As I've been working on this book, I am finding that this theme of "I'm not worthy" is somewhat common. When I'm interviewing people who are very successful, they come right out and tell me how they didn't feel like they were good enough, so they held back and didn't take action. For instance, I interviewed Tracy Enos, who is a LinkedIn Expert Advisor, and you know what was amazing about her interview?

She was super vulnerable and told me about massive failure where she was writing a book and never finished it. Here's her story.

ROB:

Tracy, can you tell me a little bit about you?

TRACY:

Sure; for starters, I am a LinkedIn Expert Advisor. I'm also a single mom of four and a grandmother of two. I've been in marketing and sales, gosh, since my first job. I never thought of it this way, but my first job was at a pizza place called Round Table Pizza, one of those old-fashioned, family-style pizza places. I learned the art of the upsell there. Then I became a hostess at an Italian restaurant, so I learned the art of selling from an early age but didn't really know it.

I started out my marketing and sales career formally in Branson, Missouri, as a timeshare salesperson. I'm telling you, that's no fun. I only lasted a few years in the business, and then in 2002, I got a real estate license and spent the bulk of my career in the mortgage and real estate industries. I learned early on that you had to look for out-of-the-box ways to market.

I didn't go to college, and I don't have a degree in marketing or business. I've learned in the trenches over the years, because social media and the tools that we have to get our message out have changed so much. I learned a lot from online programs that I subscribed to. I paid out of my own pocket for that education so I could learn to sell more and market better.

I really began to understand the psychology of selling. People buy with emotion. You have to be able to resolve a need.

So, I learned to use those tools, but more importantly, I learned how to use systems. I was in the Navy for a short amount of time, and the military works well because they have systems. Systems are key. McDonald's is a great example. They have probably one of the best systems in the world for running their franchises. So, anyway, I learned to adopt systems. If you have a system and it's a repeatable process, you're gonna make money.

ROB:

I like it. Sounds good to me. So, what have you done in your life where you decided, you planned, but you didn't take action, and what was that consequence?

TRACY:

I went to a marketing seminar, Publish and Profit, in September of 2014. That's where I met Mike Koenigs, Ed Rush, Paul Colligan, and Pam Hendrickson. The first day, I was chosen for a seven-minute hot seat. Those four totally dissected my business.

They said, "You know LinkedIn. This is what you need to do. Fire all the rest of your clients, and just do LinkedIn." Well, that was a big feat. I always thought about writing a book, but, like most people, I didn't know how to go about it.

I was approached by one of the people at the event, and we started writing a book. We pre-released the book and it became a number one bestseller, but sadly the book was never published. We pulled the book from Amazon. I could have moved forward, but I was afraid that the book would suck. I didn't know what I was doing. I've always had a fear of failure, so I've probably been the best-kept secret in the last six years in the LinkedIn world because I was hiding. I was afraid of being seen and letting people know I'm really good.

I don't know where that mindset came from, but fear handicapped me. So that's where I planned, and I failed.

ROB:

When the book didn't come out, what happened?

TRACY:

I lost business. I let down the people who knew the book was coming out, because they never received a copy. So I went back into my hole all over again. The buzz had been out there, and everybody was looking forward to it. In fact, I even had a big deal with a guy where I was going to train his whole organization of classic car dealers on how to use LinkedIn. Because that book never came out, I looked like a fool. The book was a representation of authority and expertise that never got published. I probably lost a high-six-figure deal.

ROB:

That's huge. So because of fear, you lost a high-six-figure, potentially even seven-figure deal.

TRACY:

Correct.

ROB:

Devastating. Wow.

TRACY:

Very devastating. Ed Rush told me over a year ago, before I started really writing on LinkedIn, "You need to open up about your life. You need to be vulnerable. You have to let people in." So I did, and that was probably the hardest article I've ever written.

ROB:

Right, I bet. You are absolutely amazing, by the way. When did you start working so closely with LinkedIn?

TRACY:

Thank you, Rob; it's been a journey. I started my LinkedIn career over six years ago. Unfortunately, in July of 2015, I had a bad accident and sustained third-degree burns, which landed me in the hospital for six days. I had five surgeries in nine months, and I actually went through a bout of depression and anxiety because of the burns. I gained a lot of weight, and I hibernated. If it had not been for LinkedIn and the foundation that I had already created, my business probably would have folded. I might have lost my home, but because of those foundations, I kept my head above water and a roof over our head. In the following year, I took serious action and made more money in six months using LinkedIn than I'd made in the previous eighteen months. Even though the book didn't get published, I was really having a great year with LinkedIn. I had written some *Newsfeed* posts that went viral, and it generated business for me. We're talking something that took me ten minutes to do, and because I had that foundation, it was just simple for me.

So you can understand the magnitude of the third-degree burns, let me share what happened. It was a Tuesday morning at 5:30

a.m. Unfortunately, I remember it very vividly. I was making a pot of brown rice noodles. I had overfilled it. I was barefoot, trying not to wake anybody in the house. When I took the overfilled pot to drain, it started to slosh. To avoid pouring boiling water on my feet, I jumped out of the way, but when I did that, the pot started spilling more. I tried to make it to the sink. The colander wasn't stable, and when the pot hit the colander, it all came back at me, every bit of that huge pot of boiling water and noodles. It was horrible. Horrible, horrible, horrible.

I got thrown in the cold shower for twenty minutes with all my clothes on, to stop the progression of the burns, or so we thought. I was freezing. Then I went to the emergency room. The pain was so incredibly painful, I don't even know how to explain that; even though they had given me morphine and Demerol, I couldn't stop vomiting because it was so painful.

The doctor tried to clean my skin before he wrapped me up, and I almost punched the man. That's how painful it was. He said, "In three days, you need to contact your general practitioner." At the point, we didn't know if there were going to be third-degree burns because it was all blistered.

I walked into my doctor's office, and she took one look at me and said, "Tracy, I can't clean this up. Why don't you go to the burn clinic?" I said, "Because the emergency room told me not to go to the burn clinic. They told me to come to you." She said, "Huh... I'm calling the burn clinic right now."

She got me in the very next morning. It was rough. I couldn't take pain medication because I had to drive myself. My son, Asher was with me, but at fifteen, he was too young to drive.

They cleaned me up. All the blisters had popped, and they were trying to see the damage underneath my arm. Meanwhile, I was in tears, it was so awful.

ROB:

Okay. You don't have to go into more detail because I'm already in tears, just thinking about what you—my friend—went through. I burned myself recently, just a small burn from grabbing a baking tray out of the oven without gloves on, and so I'm imagining what that would be like amplified a hundred times. Wow... I'm sorry you had to go through that. Okay, let's focus on your win. Even though that happened, you decided that nothing was going to stop you, and you moved forward.

TRACY:

Yeah, I moved forward. In October of 2015, when I was still hibernating behind my computer, I got a message from Ed asking me to manage his LinkedIn, and I actually sold a $3,000 coaching contract while doped up on morphine, my second day in the hospital. I don't recommend doing that, but it's what kept my head above water.

Ed became a client, and I wrote my very first publisher article that went viral. That landed me some more clients, so I had a nice five-figure month, which kept me going for a while.

I took a stance and decided I was going to write this damn book already. "I'm going to write it. I'm going to write it."

After I brainstormed the outline of my book, I paid somebody to take me through the process of asking me questions for each chapter, and then we got it transcribed.

We were supposed to release it in August of 2016, but it didn't happen. I got set back again, and then I made a bunch of lame-ass excuses. Here I had a mostly finished book, and business was great—no complaints there—but I still didn't get a book out. The thing is, I knew the book would actually be that one tool that would propel my business.

About a year later, 2017, I was invited to speak about LinkedIn at the big GKIC Info Summit, and this was when I decided that I was going to take action. There were no excuses anymore.

I wanted to walk onto that stage as a bestselling author, and I wasn't going to let anything stop me, so I started working on the book again. I created a campaign, did what I needed to do and uploaded the manuscript onto Amazon. Within twenty-four hours, without even actually promoting the book, I was a bestselling author.

Don't ask me how. I don't even know. It must've been the topic, but I've been number one for five months without promotion, and I'm still taking action every single day.

Because of this book, I now have six speaking engagements. Three of them are paid so far. I've landed numerous clients because of this book.

I decided that I was going to finish this damn book, and I took action. It had to be rewritten, because LinkedIn completely changed their user interface and a lot of the strategies had changed when using publisher in writing articles. I didn't want to write some crappy little book; I wanted to overdeliver, full of great tips and juicy tidbits. I'm under a very strict deadline, and I'm making it happen. By the time your book is out, mine will be finished.

When it is complete, I know that it's going to land me even more clients, probably more than I can handle, so I've already set up a team. I took action. I was told that I needed to have a team in order to grow my business and stop being a solo entrepreneur, so I did. I hired the team last week.

ROB:

Thank you for being so candid and sharing your story.

TRACY:

Thank you.

I've probably said this a few times by now, but I am so grateful to be surrounded by authentic people who aren't afraid to share their stories to demonstrate the power of the Law of Action. You just have to remember that you can overcome incredible odds. Ask for help, and keep going.

Another awesome friend of mine, Tina Williams, took some time to let me interview her. What she shared with me was so incredible. I realized another common theme among powerful, successful people is that they give so much to other people that they forget to take care of themselves!

Here's how that went.

ROB:

All right, Tina. Let's talk about you!

TINA:

Well, I'm a mother of four daughters. That's my predominant job and the job that I love the most. I'd say other than my girls, my students are the biggest reflection of my success. It has been a joy to watch people become bestselling authors, top product creators, local business consultants, shop owners, and coaches after they work with me and implement my "no fail" implementation strategies. My goal has always been to inspire, motivate and educate people to find their own personal greatness and turn their talent into profit.

ROB:

So, definitely an entrepreneur.

TINA:

Yep. Since I was fourteen, I've always had businesses. I started out working for people who had horses, braiding manes and tails and cleaning stalls. That was my first entrepreneurial job. I am a serial entrepreneur with multiple businesses. I currently have a social media certification business, an online marketing business, and a cannabis business.

ROB:

Cannabis seems to be really growing as a healing medicine. Tell me about that.

TINA:

I run a health and wellness business, which predominantly sells hemp products. CBD is the same as hemp, and it doesn't have enough THC in it to create a psychoactive effect or "high." Cannabis is the name of the plant, which has several parts that can be used for different things. When you hear the word "hemp," it refers to any cannabis product from a plant with under .3 percent THC. I work with CBD, or hemp oil, so there is no regulation on it.

And then I had a series of three strokes in three months. Thanks to that experience, I changed my entire life. I reinvented myself, and now I'm running a business where I can help people every single day. I'm really excited about that and all the businesses that I've had despite all the troubles and tribulations of doing them.

ROB:

I hear you on that! Wow, to recover from three strokes is in no way an easy feat. One thing that I know about you, Tina, is that you are not a victim. You are a true action taker. What is something that you did where you used the Law of Action? A time when you decided, planned, acted, and had a miraculous, incredible result?

TINA:

Back when I had my first online marketing business, I worked with a partner. We decided to do what we called the "social media certification business," which at the time was very new— so new, in fact, that we were the very first ones who actually got Google behind us.

ROB:

Wow. What year was this?

TINA:

Around 2011, when social media really started rolling. It was the infancy of Facebook particularly, which became more of a platform for networking when it went public in 2012. Twitter, Instagram, Pinterest, Snapchat...few people knew about those. So we decided to do a social media certification course, because I had done a book on Twitter and people loved it. We built a list of people who wanted to help local businesses learn how to use Facebook, Twitter, and LinkedIn. Those were the big three that were catching on, so it was great timing.

We decided to do a ninety-minute webinar. We ended up with about 900 people on the call. I was freaking out, absolutely scared to death! The biggest thing for me was that social media was so new. What made me an expert? Who the heck was I to say that I'm an expert, that I could teach people how to make an income learning and selling Facebook, Twitter, and LinkedIn? I really didn't know who I was or how I could have deserved to be able to do that. My partner had a lot of confidence, and we decided to throw all caution into the wind and just do it. We put together a killer course, pitched it to these 900 people, and at the end of the webinar all we heard was cha ching, cha ching, cha ching! We had 104 people join at $2,000 apiece! So we decided, we put a plan together, we took killer action, and we had amazing success based on one ninety-minute webinar that netted $200,000.

There were a couple of glitches, but we got through it. We had set a goal of 100 people joining the course at $2,000 each, and we did it!

ROB:

If you had decided and made that plan but never had the courage to act, you would've lost out on the start of your business, and over $200,000 of income after one ninety-minute webinar.

TINA:

Yes. Basically, this was like a catalyst with a snowball effect. Not only did we sell $200,000 worth of a course, we had over 100 people in the course who did so tremendously well that we continued to make courses over the next year and put together a nearly seven-figure business, all based on this one webinar that I somehow thought I didn't deserve to be on. If I didn't take action, I not only would've lost probably more than one million dollars on this one decision that I made, but I would not have built the influence that I had, and I wouldn't have met you, Rob.

ROB:

Awwww.

TINA:

It's true. We got so popular with our courses and training. Our testimonials from people who worked with us got us invited to speak at events, and that's where I met you. If I hadn't taken action, I wouldn't have the pleasure of being in your book, because I wouldn't have met the amazing Rob Actis.

ROB:

Oh, you're so sweet, Tina.

TINA:

People are important. Connecting is so important. Without it, I wouldn't be where I am today because I wouldn't have met the people I've met. As a matter of fact, I met my business partner through an event that I was speaking at, so if I didn't make that decision, I wouldn't know who I know, I wouldn't be where I am today, and it would've changed the entire course of my life. I probably wouldn't even live in Florida.

ROB:

It's quite a journey, isn't it? I know you have been a powerful leader for your students. Was there ever a time when you didn't take action and missed out?

TINA:

I have pain every day over this one. Two of my friends have an amazing online course that teaches you how to do print-on-demand products and sell them on Amazon, eBay, and Etsy. Because I was friends with them, I promoted their course to my group of people, and I actually did a subsequent course to help my coaching students do well in that particular product and make money with it.

I put together my plan to help people make six figures, yet I personally never took action. I kick myself every day, because many of those coaching students that I helped make that plan with are making six figures and beyond. And their lives are changing, but mine isn't.

ROB:

So you didn't take action to actually do what you were coaching other people to do.

TINA:

Right. I think that falls back to my fear of not being worthy. Sometimes I'm a little bit of a procrastinator, and sometimes I think things through way too much. It's amazing how sometimes we can tell other people what to do, but we don't take action ourselves.

ROB:

Wow, what do you think you lost?

TINA:

I have students who are literally making six figures minimum. I have one student who made $300,000 dollars last year, just doing that print-on-demand courses, following the exact plan that I created. It's incredible.

ROB:

Well, I think you are simply amazing, Tina; even with that setback, you have accomplished a lot. I'm sure there are many choices I could have made that would have interrupted our meeting, but for some reason, we did meet. I'm grateful to call you my friend.

TINA:

Thanks so much, Rob.

If you decide, based on fear, that you are not going to do something, and you miss out on an amazing experience or opportunity, whose fault is it?

Whose fault is it that you don't succeed in that way? There's no way to push the blame away from yourself.

It's your fault. Don't miss the shot by not taking it.

Decide, Plan, Act.

Never let fear stop you.

When it's Motivation that's Lacking

What if you aren't afraid, just unmotivated?

Using the Law of Action to Get Motivated

- **Decide:** Finding motivation means admitting that you aren't motivated yet, and you are ready to change that. It's really about personal responsibility. Your life is where it is as a result of every action you have taken, or not taken. Don't beat yourself up over this, just notice where you are and start from there. If you are deciding to "get motivated," you'll have to figure out why you haven't been before and change that behavior. Before you go to the planning step, be sure this decision is something you are ready for.

- **Plan:** Accountability will help turn self-motivation into a new habit. Find a partner who is also ready to be more motivated into taking action toward their goals and check in daily. The tide will rise, and all ships rise with it. Find people who are more motivated than you, and rise with them. Find simple things you know you should do but don't, like flossing your teeth and making your bed, and think about why you do or should do those things. For instance, flossing keeps your teeth healthier and less prone to cavities and other painful, expensive setbacks. When you know your why, motivation comes much easier.

- **Act:** Set yourself up for success by starting simple. As easy as it is to make your bed, do you do it? This is a great way to begin working with a partner and check in with each other without getting overwhelmed. Once this becomes a habit, add another action to do every day. Maybe...working out, meditating, journaling, doing the dishes or even making the bed?

For the last ten years, I have made my bed every day. I know it sounds funny, because I even make my bed when I'm traveling and staying in a hotel, where I don't have to. It's not about cleanliness, organization, or getting into a made bed. It's about starting my day in action.

It's rare, but sometimes I don't make my bed right away when I get up. It's interesting because it is a barometer for how I'm feeling, and I am aware of it and take action to feel better. I know that when I don't make my bed, I need to take time to check in with myself and see what's going on.

Once I figure that out and take care of it, I make my bed, even if it isn't until the evening.

How do you get into the habit of making your bed every day? Use the Law of Action. Decide, Plan, Act. It's the simplest way to get motivated.

Before you go to bed at night, set the intention to make your bed the next day. When you wake up, make your bed. It really can be that simple.

Make new habits by starting small and adding additional ones weekly.

You might find yourself accomplishing something you never thought you could do at all, and actually knocking it out of the park! For instance, here I am, writing a book on the Law of Action.

Am I afraid? Honestly, there is some fear in doing this. It's my first book, and I'm learning a lot as I go. The thing is, I'm using any fear that comes up to fuel me and challenge me instead of shutting me down.

Here's a funny thing that happened.

My sister, Anita, is one of the most amazing women in the world. I love her dearly. We have the kind of relationship that's honest and open, and we talk pretty often.

The last time I was in San Diego, I stopped by to see her and told her I was writing this book. She asked what it was about, and I described the Law of Action.

Her response was, "Oh, that's perfect for you, Rob! That's great! You do so much in your life, it makes sense to share your story. But..."

Then there was a pause.

She looked at me sort of...seriously, and said, "Wait... You're writing a book? You can't even write!"

Now, she didn't say that to be mean. She was saying that because she helped raise me growing up, and I'd had a really difficult time writing. She looked genuinely concerned.

Then I smiled at her and asked her what I was really good at. After a split second, she said, "You can talk!"

Oh yes, I can talk.

If you can talk, you can write a book. It's a process, and I'm finding out it is a lot of work. It takes a team to pull it all together. I've been an MC for years and in all my public speaking, I've always talked to my audiences about taking action. Even when I radio personality, I talked about taking action! I've always been the action guy; it's who I am at my core. I've shared the Law of Action verbally my whole life, and I realized that if I could speak it, it could and should be a book. Maybe you can or maybe you can't tell by reading this, but most of this book was spoken into a microphone, then transcribed, edited, rewritten and arranged so that you can hold it in your hands. If you're listening to the audiobook, you're getting it in a similar way to how I originally spoke it.

Interesting, isn't it?

At first, the whole thing was really scary. Honestly, I was scared out of my mind because I don't consider myself to be a writer, but I do see myself as a communicator. And here it is again: "Why not me?"

It occurred to me that I had already been preparing to write my own book. The books I needed to read showed up in my life as narration projects. As a voice actor, I have been the narrator for many books, but not just ANY random books: the perfect books that led me to where I am today.

For example, I was chosen to narrate Hal Elrod's book, *The Miracle Morning*. As I read it aloud and recorded it for the audio book, my life changed. I decided to actually do his Miracle Morning 30-Day Challenge.

I used to sleep in every morning, then roll out of bed half-awake and start my day. I still worked a lot—and worked hard—but I wasn't a morning person. I stayed up late and slept late. *The Miracle Morning* is all about reprogramming yourself to jumpstart your day with a great morning routine. By the time I finished narrating it, something strange had happened. Just by narrating it and, of course, following the principles, I'd become a morning person!

Since that book, I've narrated many others that have changed my life. You probably won't be surprised to hear that Honorée Corder's *You Must Write a Book* was a huge catalyst in *The Law of Action* coming into reality and actually becoming a book.

As her narrator, she has coached me along the way about the ins and outs of being an author. She has shared her stories. With her wisdom, I have gained tools to create a great book of my own.

Everybody wins!

The books I have been narrating for several years now have given me a great foundation. As people listened to the audio books I've done, they began to tell ME that I should write a book.

I was inspired by Hal Elrod, I was inspired by Honorée Corder, and I was inspired by the people who have encouraged me to write a book. Here it is.

I overcame my fear of writing a book. I overcame my feelings of unworthiness and self-doubt. You can do the same.

Now, thinking back on all of the things that I went through to get to this place, I'm humbled.

Decide, Plan, Act.

If I hadn't gone through with that Bayer Aspirin job, my life would have taken a different turn.

It opened doors for me. A whole new world opened up, actually, and a wealth of opportunity fell right into my lap.

Looking back, it's amazing that I was trying to stop myself.

Looking back, I'm glad Anthony, my agent, didn't force me, and let me decide.

Looking back, the struggle was real, and going through it was worthwhile.

I hope the next time you get in that type of situation—where you're staring adversity in the face and feeling hopeless—that you will think of what the consequences could be for either choice: pushing forward or giving up.

This is an abundant world and universe we live in. There's enough for everyone. You have to make the conscious choice to take action, and it's all out there waiting for you when you do.

On Intuition and Taking Chances

A more recent action I took was to experience Ed Rush's Ultimate Breakthrough event. It's a three-day event that I decided to take a chance on.

My intuition nudged me to do it, and I'm so glad I did.

I go to lots of events, and many are designed to inspire and fire up the crowd, get the energy flowing.

This wasn't like that. A couple of things happened during that event that changed my life immediately.

One exercise we did was to write down the one thing that was holding us back in our lives. One thing that the voice in our head keeps repeating so much that it limits our success and ability to take action.

We wrote it down on a little piece of paper and put it in our pocket.

Then there was this incredible presenter, Melodee Meyer, who came up and spoke. She's a martial arts expert, an incredible entrepreneur, and just an amazing woman.

After her highly motivational speech, she said, "Everybody reach into your pockets and pull out the piece of paper you wrote on. Now, look at that piece of paper and then take the board that is coming to you and write the one thing that is holding you back on it."

They handed out these wood boards; you can see mine in the photograph below. The message I wrote on my board was, "I'm not worthy."

On the other side, we wrote the opposite: "I'm worthy." When I wrote those words, I looked at them for a moment and felt how much I had let those feelings of unworthiness block what was really true.

I am worthy.

I AM WORTHY!

I felt something inside of me stir.

I also understood the symbolism of what we were gonna do.

We were gonna break these freaking boards. And they were thick. Strong, like the thought of "I'm not worthy" had been for so long. One by one, the group brought their boards up and, under her direction, they broke them.

I have a background in martial arts. I made it to a purple belt, but I'd never broken a board. It was not something that we did in our dojo, but I knew the power of breaking boards. I knew the power of focusing your energy and breaking something bigger and stronger than you'd ever thought you could.

Since I broke that board, an immense amount of energy has been unleashed. I kept the board, because it reminds me of breaking free of the "I'm not worthy" lie.

I am taking action in ways that I never thought I'd take action before, and I am following the Law of Action, repeating the cycle more and more often. Decide, Plan, Act.

Yes, I had an Ultimate Breakthrough.

The event was amazing. It launched me forward and challenged me to take on enormous tasks, like actually finish writing this book. I'm grateful, and sometimes exhausted, but you know what? It's all worth it.

The year of 2017 was enormously transformative for me. I've learned to come back to myself, what I need, and what my purpose is.

I've asked for help, and now I work with amazing people who are good at the stuff I am terrible at. I follow the Law of Action, and I have found my flow. That's an interesting story, something I never expected.

 Take a moment, and pause.

Things to think about:

- How do you talk to yourself? Would you hang out with some-one who talks to you like you talk to yourself?

- What would it take for you to realize you are worthy?

- How can you ask for help to take action so you don't miss the shot?

Chapter 5

LET IT FLOW, LET IT FLOW, LET IT FLOW

"Just remember, you can do anything you set your mind to, but it takes action, perseverance, and facing your fears."

-GILLIAN ANDERSON

AS SOMEONE WHO LIKES TO TAKE ACTION, I have learned to admit when I can't do the tasks necessary to take the action. When that happens, I ask for help.

I've gotten really good at delegating and allowing other people to do what they are good at. We are all so different. I've figured out that some things I am not good at are a breeze for someone else.

To give you a little back story, I have ADD. I get side-tracked very easily—all the time, in fact. This can be useful in creative situations, or when multitasking, but it doesn't keep my life organized. On the contrary, it creates chaos.

I am divorced. Divorce is hard, but you can survive it. One of the things that happened after my divorce is that life became very chaotic.

What my life had been, as a husband, radically shifted when I began to live alone again.

I essentially had to reinvent myself, and the challenges in my life really became clear.

I will take a moment to acknowledge Nikki, my ex-wife, for keeping our home in order. Thank you, Nikki, for dealing with my clutter and keeping things managed. You were really good at it.

After we were no longer married, I had to figure out how to create that order on my own. But how?

As I healed from the divorce, I looked at the state of my life. I looked at how my house was and I looked at the situation that I was in, and then the Law of Action kicked in again. I knew I needed help to get things back on track.

Decide. Plan. Act.

Using the Law of Action to Get Help

- **Decide:** I decided I needed to restore my peace, and I knew I had no idea how. All I knew was that it was time, and it had to happen. I imagined living in my home with it feeling like a hotel. I wanted a place for everything and everything in its place. I saw it and felt it in my mind.

- **Plan:** I sent a message to the universe asking to be guided in getting this result. I had no idea what it meant; I only knew I couldn't do it alone. My "Plan" was to surrender and allow the right help to show up.

- **Act:** Within the next week, I met someone who would change my life. I didn't know what would happen, but I KNEW that she was the one I had asked for. I acted. I asked her, and I hired her! My action resulted in massive changes in my life.

The way I had used the Law of Action that time was not to be in control of the situation, but to know that I had no idea how to do it and ask for help. This is miraculous stuff. I was in a social setting when I met Andrea King. She's a super cool lady, with these amazing dreadlocks and incredible energy. I was immediately curious about her, but I had no idea that she was the one I'd asked for. I had forgotten about my request. I had let it go.

I asked what she did, and she sort of smiled and responded, "A lot of things."

Then she told me that she has a company called Flowganize.

"Flowganize? What the heck is Flowganize?" I was intrigued.

She described it like this:

"I work with people who are looking for decluttering and organizing, but in an unusual way. We look at WHY you create the chaos, then work through those issues so you can let them go and live in peace. The clutter and chaos goes away along with it. It's also Feng Shui and energy rebalancing."

Something felt a lot different than the organizers I had tried in the past. She talked about flow, and chaos and clarity, and calm and peace and harmony. I was like, "Yes. I want that. Yes. Yes. Yes."

All I knew was that I was a definite YES, so I gave her a shot and hired her.

She came to my house a couple of days later. I showed her my chaos. She quietly observed my home for a bit while I talked about it and shared my story.

She didn't seem bothered at all by my home and the aftermath of the divorce that I hadn't yet gotten under control. She just said, "I got this. You'll be okay."

I felt relief immediately, and we discussed how things would go. She told me it wouldn't be easy, but it would be worth it. I was ready. I was also nervous.

What happened after that was something I can't even explain.

She didn't just do all the organizing work and then bail. She looked at the big picture and helped me understand why things were so un-organized. Then she did the unthinkable: she asked to see my garage.

The garage had become the dumping ground for all of the stuff I didn't want to deal with. When I opened the door into it, I felt vulnerable and hoped she wouldn't run away.

She asked if I wanted to be able to put my car in the garage. I looked at her like she was nuts and said, "That would be amazing."

Andrea nodded. "Then this is the starting point."

Since then, Andrea has been working with me, being good at what she does so I can be good at what I do. She's one of my dearest friends, and she knows everything about me. I have a hard time describing what she does, but the results are real.

My life has changed. She has challenged me to face myself in ways I had avoided for a long time.

She has validated me for the things I am good at and helped me to see and get support for my blind spots and weaknesses.

It's been hard, sometimes really hard, but you know what? She was right; it was worth it.

She is the right help for me. I thought I needed an organizer, but it turned out I needed a Flowganizer.

I'm just going to say: thank you, Andrea. I tell her that a lot. I really don't understand how it all works, but I am grateful every day for the life I am now living. I feel like I live in a hotel, just like I wanted. My car is even in the garage! After I had been Flowganized on a weekly basis for a while, I noticed I smiled more. My house was flowing, and I was starting to flow. I was becoming a different person, a little more each week.

It was mind-blowing how different I was becoming. I was spending my time with great people, doing remarkable things.

When I talked about these changes I noticed, Andrea would tell me, "You're in your flow. Good job. You attract what you are."

Sometimes you know those things, and then you hear them in a new way and really KNOW them.

"You attract what you are."

Andrea helped me get my life into flow—she totally Flowganized me—as much as Jason helped me transform my body. I do well with people who hold me accountable.

I asked Andrea for an interview for this book to share more of her experiences. I know her pretty well, but she revealed some things about herself that I didn't expect. Here's how that went.

ROB:

So I know you as the amazing Flowganizer, but I want to talk about your experiences today. In this book, *The Law of Action*, I'm asking people who have influenced my life to answer a couple of questions, if that would be okay?

ANDREA:

Of course!

ROB:

Well, let's get into it. With the Law of Action in mind, what great accomplishment have you achieved after you have made the decision to do it, planned how to do it, and then taken action?

ANDREA:

I got a horse.

ROB:

An actual horse?

ANDREA:

Yes. My dream horse. A black-and-white tobiano paint horse, to be exact! I was the little girl who wanted a pony her whole life. I dreamed of horses and collected statues and posters and figurines and anything related to horses. I read a zillion books about horses. When I was twenty-one, I worked at a beautiful breeding barn in Iowa for a summer, cleaning up poop and caring for the horses. I loved it all. I spent my whole life knowing someday I'd have a horse. I was patient and passionate about it. I always had a bit of my focus there.

ROB:

So you decided really early; when did you begin to plan for it?

ANDREA:

Logistically, I couldn't have a horse until conditions were right for it. It's a lot more of a commitment than adopting a puppy. I didn't want to board; I wanted property. I wanted to do it right. I imagined looking out of my window and seeing a horse in my backyard. I spent years imagining it, actually.

ROB:

So your Plan phase took a while, but it seems like you knew what you were doing.

ANDREA:

Yeah. I learned to be patient with it. Sometimes it was really hard to wait.

I was a veterinary technician for several years, and the owner of the clinic is a horseman, so I got closer to horses again. One day, we hired a new manager who happened to be a paint horse breeder. He and I were having lunch one day and started talking about horses. I told him about my dream horse.

ROB:

And...there it is!

ANDREA:

Yeah, I still get a little emotional remembering it. He had a yearling stud colt, a registered paint horse, black and white tobiano. This was in 2005. What's funny is that I was twenty-nine at that point, and I sort of pulled the trigger on deciding that it was time. I had declared, "I WILL HAVE A HORSE BEFORE I AM THIRTY!" That lunch happened about three weeks after I said that out loud.

ROB:

So not only did he have your dream horse, he was willing to sell it?

ANDREA:

Yep. I arranged to go over and see the colt. It was the year that we got tons of rain in February. He had a shaggy winter coat and was super muddy. I fell madly in love. I was giddy, elated, and I went home to my husband and told him about the colt. He pulled me out of my overexcited state back down to Earth so we could talk about it and figure out how it could work. Within a week, I had signed the papers, bought my horse, and named him Mojo!

ROB:

That is an amazing story! How did your life change after having a horse?

ANDREA:

Mojo was basically a big baby, but because I got him before I became a mom, it was a lot of new responsibility. I just treated him like a big dog for a while. I spent a lot of time with him. I kept him at my manager's house, which was close to the clinic, so I went over before and after work, and also at lunch.

Not long after that, we bought a property with room for horses, a sweet 1.25-acre place.

The thing about horses is they're like potato chips; you can't just have one!

Seriously, though, they're herd animals, so I got Mojo a companion goat for a while. Over the next several years, I had two human children and was given two more horses that needed homes. One has gone on to be a trail horse, so I have two now. Mojo is twelve and lives in my backyard with his current companion, Rain. She's a little chestnut mare who arrived on my daughter's seventh birthday. Lucky kid! The best part is looking out of my window and seeing horses in my backyard.

ROB:

Your dream came true! I never knew that about you. That's a great example of Decide, Plan, Act. Sometimes it takes more time to manifest what we dream of.

ANDREA:

That's my most satisfying example. I have definitely manifested a lot of things that were amazing, and some that weren't...

ROB:

Can you think something in your life that you decided you wanted but never followed through on it?

ANDREA:

Oh, sure, plenty of times. I have "brilliant ideas" all the time. I used to start throwing ideas together and making plans immediately on just about every idea that came up. Obviously, that doesn't work. What I've learned is that we all can do lots of things, but the key is to hone in on what we are really good at. I teach Feng Shui, organization, and decluttering, but the real thing I am doing is helping people find their focus and superpowers. I had to do it for myself first. I have a trail of business cards for things that never went anywhere. Brilliant ideas that weren't meant to be.

ROB:

Do you think you bailed on them because you got stuck, or...?

ANDREA:

It's more like the initial excitement faded, and I got hit with the reality that I was pushing instead of flowing. We just aren't supposed to pursue EVERY idea we have. I learned about how stubbornly I could pursue something that wasn't going to work. It's all an awesome learning process, really.

ROB:

So when you think about the Law of Action, do you relate to it?

ANDREA:

Definitely. It creates motion and flow. It allows things to happen. I really like the emphasis on failure, honestly! I'm an expert at failure, so I can coach and support my clients when they experience it.

ROB:

Andrea, on a personal note, you have helped me in so many ways to get where I am today. What advice would you give me, or any other client, relating to the Law of Action?

ANDREA:

Respect divine timing. That's it. If it took you many years to create your life of chaos, it will not be undone overnight, but it can be undone. Be patient with your own timelines and processes. My methods with Flowganize, or yours with the Law of Action, both create forward movement. It doesn't have to be earth-shattering and devastating. Even small movement is still movement. I see your concept as a version of mindfulness that keeps your life moving. It's simple, and it's needed. Even if life slows down or speeds up, just keep following the cycle.

OH! One more thing, I guess. Let go of stuff from the past to make room for your next level. Emotions, attitudes, and physical STUFF that don't work with who you are now have to go. That's a thing.

After that interview, I reflected on who I'd been when I met Andrea and how much I have since changed my ways of being.

I've learned to cook, do my laundry (most of the time), and—I guess some call it "adulting"—but I have become okay with taking care of myself.

I can't hide anymore. I have become a better version of Rob, and I attract people who reflect that to me. Wow.

Speaking of reflections, I met another amazing woman almost three years ago who I adore deeply: Tanya.

She's my amazing girlfriend, best friend, and partner.

When I met Andrea, I had been with Tanya for over six months and we were getting along well, but I don't know if our relationship would have deepened the way it has if I had not gone through my Flowganize experience. Flowganize was not something that just cleared my house; it cleared *me*. It helped me become a better person.

Tanya and I have a relationship that just flows. Things are easy because we are committed to communication. From the first moment I saw her, I took action.

Using the Law of Action to Meet Someone New

- **Decide:** I am interested in getting to know that person. I am attracted to them on some level and curious about them. I am going to initiate a connection.

- **Plan:** I will walk across the room and say hello. I will express my interest in getting to know them. I know that I may get rejected, but I am okay with it as long as I try.

> • **Act:** I'm taking a deep breath to center my energy, then walking over and saying hello. I have no expectation of a result.

If I didn't take the action to walk over and say hello, I would not be able to call Tanya my girlfriend today.

Was I nervous? Maybe a little, but planning and preparing without expectation allows for whatever is going to happen to just...happen. Being in the present without worrying makes room for incredible things to happen.

With my near-death experiences, I have learned to cherish the time I have with people I care about and be present in the moment.

If I was to give any relationship advice, it would be this: live in the moment. Be present with the person in front of you as if it's the last day you'll have with them.

Sure, we have to plan our days and make appointments to take care of life. At times we do have to think about the past and future, but it takes awareness to live in the present moment. Tanya and I focus on that as much as possible, and it takes a lot of the stress and the strain out of our time together. We just really let our relationship flow. We connect. We talk about how we feel. We share openly and honestly.

How did we get to that level of connection?

We practiced. A lot. We also completely let go of worrying about what the other would think of us and just showed up as we are. No apologies, no holding back. Complete transparency. What a concept!

Is it always perfect? Nope. But we have agreed to take time to communicate when we have a disagreement or conflict. It takes awareness to hear each other and not have to be right. We've learned to do that, so we can get back to what's important in our relationship.

This has allowed us to be highly present with each other, and we're incredibly clear in our communication with each other about...well, everything.

Taking Action Toward Amazing Relationships

Early on in our relationship, Tanya and I attended an event together that really helped us learn to open up, connect, and communicate.

Don't laugh, don't judge, but these events are called..."Cuddle Parties." Yes, they are a real thing.

It took me a bit not to judge and laugh myself, but once I understood the purpose and value of them, I was hooked.

Everybody needs connection, yet very few people—especially singles—know how to get it.

The culture of the Cuddle Party is about crystal-clear communication, asking for what you want, and saying "yes" or "no" to others who are asking for what they want. During an event, there is time to practice this verbal communication, and it's all guided. Then there is actual, nurturing touch. Hugs, back rubs, foot rubs, and cuddling. It's a safe, non-sexual space where people can get the touch and affection they crave.

There are Cuddle Party facilitators who host and guide the group through a series of exercises and communications. You can check them out at CuddleParty.com and find one near you if you're interested.

One of the key things that I love about Cuddle Parties, which I'm so thankful that I've learned is, "No means no, maybe means no, and you only say yes if you're a hell yes."

If you can learn those three guidelines, you can not only identify when to take action in your life (hint: when it's a hell yes!) but have extraordinary relationships as well.

I've experienced improved communication not only in personal relationships, but also in my business relationships. Crystal-clear communication. If you are wondering about something, ask. What's the worst that can happen? You might get a "no." So you learn to hear "no" and not take it personally.

Tanya and I have an agreement that we are 100 percent open and honest with our yeses and nos, and our maybes are always nos. I get to be me, and she gets to be her.

Every day, Tanya gets the choice to be with me, and every day I get the choice to be with her. So far, every day for almost three years, we have chosen each other.

We let it flow.

Notice the relationships you have in your life. Notice how you feel around people. Do your relationships flow?

Every relationship is a choice. Choose how you spend your time and energy wisely. They say time is money. I see that time is energy and currency, which is much like money. Why would anyone waste any of those resources?

"Act"ing Your Way into More Monetary Wealth

Speaking of money...

How is your relationship with cash these days?

That's a big one for a lot of people. How would you like for money to flow in and out of your life easily? Imagine never worrying if there's enough, just knowing it's there, flowing in and out, allowing you to live life comfortably.

What if for every dollar you spent, three times as much came back in?

What a great concept!

Guess what? It's real, and to finish the chapter on flow, I'm going to give you a hint about bringing money into your life.

I just recently finished narrating a new series of books called *Magic Money*, including the titles *Beginning Magic Money*, *Advanced Magic Money*, and *Magic Money Mastery*. As I was reading them, I spoke to the author, Holly Alexander.

We talked about letting money circulate in your life. It's about letting it flow out and then letting it flow back in. Money is energy; it's called currency for a reason. It is supposed to have a flow to it.

I'd recommend reading the whole *Magic Money* series so you can get the full experience. (Or, if you're too busy to read or would just prefer to listen, you can pick up a copy of the audio book, narrated by yours truly.)

You can use the *Magic Money* series as a complement to *The Law of Action*. It all comes back to the three principles: Decide, Plan, Act.

Yes, the Law of Action applies to your money as well. Your attitude about money, your ability to let money flow, and your fear and limitation of having not enough or too much money. Yes, some people actually are afraid of having too much money; it goes back to the "I'm not worthy" mindset.

Even before reading Holly's books, I had the ability to manifest money; after adding Holly's techniques, I have amplified my manifestation. I have now implemented Holly's Magic Money principles into my life. They work. It's a mindset shift, and it's possible for you, too. Are you ready for Magic Money?

With the Law of Action AND Magic Money, you have two keys to change your financial status. If you just buy her books, and plan to follow them, but never start to read/listen to them or implement the techniques, you're missing the action step.

Decide, Plan, Act.

Using the Law of Action to Attract Money

- **Decide:** Feel the emotion of being wealthy and abundant. Imagine never hesitating to buy what you want, knowing your relationship with money is healthy and solid. Imagine opening your bank account and seeing a balance that's ten times what you are used to. Imagine opening your wallet and seeing several hundred-dollar bills in it.

- **Plan:** Choose a method to change your relationship with money. The Magic Money series by Holly Alexander or Ed Rush's The 21-Day Miracle are two amazingly powerful ways to get results. Commit to devoting time to actually DO THE WORK. Put it in your planner or calendar. Set alarms. You are reprogramming your mind, so plan a way that will work for you. Set small, measurable goals.

- **Act:** Begin following the plan you have made! Regardless of the method you use, you have to take action and put time and effort into sticking to it. Focus. Reward yourself as you go.

The ability to manifest money is just one more result you can experience when you use the Law of Action. The more easily money flows in your life, the more opportunities you have. You can try new things and even take risks in different ways. For example, almost two years ago, a surprising opportunity came up for me to become part owner of a hot rod shop, something I likely couldn't have even considered if it hadn't been for both Magic Money and the Law of Action.

In the next chapter, I'm going to talk more in-depth about the value of a team and how working with other people can accelerate your success.

I know "you can do it all yourself," but the thing is, you don't need to.

Take a moment, and pause.

Things to think about:

- What isn't flowing in your life? Relationships, money, health?

- How can you be more honest with yourself so these things can change?

- How is your relationship with money? Are you open to more of it?

Chapter 6

TAKING A RISK TO LIVE THE DREAM

"Action is the foundational key to all success."

-PABLO PICASSO

IF YOU HAD TOLD ME TEN YEARS AGO I was going to be part owner of a custom hot rod shop, I would never have believed you.

I mean, I like nice cars, but I'm not THAT into them. I like driving them and looking at them, but I have never really been interested in how they work.

As it turns out, that is working perfectly for my current business partnership. Mods Hot Rods

My partners and I at the hot rod shop exhibit some of our cars at the Goodguys car show. In 2017, we showed six of our cars.

Like I said, I don't know a lot about cars. Shawn, my partner, introduced me to another guy who had walked over and started asking me questions about a 1964 Corvette.

He got very technical and detailed, then said, "So, what do you think about that?"

I said, "To be honest with you, I really don't have an opinion, because I don't understand half of what you just said."

He was obviously confused. "Well, why not? What the hell? I heard you're one of the partners of this hot rod shop, and you don't know that about this car?"

I said, "No, I don't." I am very upfront and honest that I don't know much about cars.

He said that I was dumb, and I replied, "I'm not dumb. Being able to admit and realize the things that I don't know is actually really smart. I then surround myself with the people who *do* know those things. I will tell you, I am confident that we have one of the top teams in the country because we hire the best. I will match our techs, our body workers, our painter, and our fabricators up against anybody else. So actually, I think I'm pretty smart."

> "A fool thinks himself to be wise,
> but a wise man knows himself to be a fool."
> —Shakespeare

I'm not sure that guy got it, but my point is, you don't have to know everything. It's okay to admit you don't know everything. It's okay to ask for help because the more times you ask for help, the more easily things get done.

If you look under the hood of a car, you'll see that there are many parts to an engine, each of which has a specific function. Same with the rest of the vehicle. If you expect the steering wheel to stop the car, you'll be disappointed, because that's the brake's job. Even I know that. It's the same with people in a team. Let every gear turn the right way. Let every tire rotate, and let every fuel pump pump fuel. Let every component do its part so the machine can run smoothly.

When it comes to people, that means delegating.

In the past, I did everything by myself. Since I've learned to delegate, I now have two agents who both feed me work that's right in my wheelhouse. They send me auditions, I send them back completed. If I book the job, they get paid, and I get paid. It's teamwork.

My companies are growing because my teams are growing.

The hot rod shop is doing well because the team is solid.

Once you realize that you can't do everything and you check your ego at the door, delegate, and let people do what they do best, things flow.

I'm not very good at accounting, or office management, or scheduling, or organizing. So I found people who are, and now they do what they love, and I do what I love. It has to be a win-win.

Find the people who are smarter than you, and you will get to your goals a whole lot faster. Surround yourself with people you can learn from.

Writing this book is taking a team. Actually, it's taking a much bigger team than I expected. My sister, Anita, was right. I can't write, but I can talk, so my spoken words are being crafted into a book that will convey something I'm very passionate about.

It's not just one person sitting at a typewriter and pounding out pages; it's so much more.

Every book you see on any bookshelf has been created by a team of people: copywriters, editors, proofers, cover and layout designers, even photographers.

There is a whole army of people behind most every book. Actually, there's an army of people behind most any worthwhile venture.

And that's good news, because it means that you don't have to know everything to be successful. As a matter of fact, the most successful people have teams around them. You can still use the Law of Action.

Decide, Plan, Act.

Just don't act on everything personally. Delegation is part of the planning. Plan WHO will help, then Act by giving them the work to do.

The CEO of a major corporation doesn't do everything. They oversee things, and they have a team to implement actions. The most successful organizations, the most successful people, bring people together. They have teams.

Take my good friend Derral Eves of Creatus, for instance. He is a video marketing expert and globally known speaker and trainer who works with the top brands in business along with YouTubers around the world. He has generated over 25 billion video views and sold hundreds of millions of dollars in product through video marketing.

Derral also participated in industry conferences, but he felt a need for more in-depth events. He wanted something more engaging than panels and keynote speakers, so he created something that would not only be able to fulfill his desire for richer content, action items, and intensive training, but would also grow to be the top conference for video marketing professionals in the world.

He began with a small, private conference that he called VidSummit, where 100 video marketing experts like himself met to share their skills and help each other. He created a transparent culture of industry professionals where everyone walked away with something very tangible.

What started as a small conference grew quickly. In the audience of now over 2,000 attendees sat video creators and experts who already had millions of subscribers, sharing their expertise and learning from each other. Eight out of the ten most viral video ad creators of all time presented at the event.

One of these presenters, Jeffrey Harmon, worked alongside Derral as executive producers on a brilliant marketing video, the Squatty Potty Pooping Unicorn ad, which generated over $45 million in sales over the course of one year.

Derral's passion to bring the right people together has created a synergistic opportunity for video creators and marketers. He watched as a more diversified group of creators and marketers gathered, networked, and worked together, sometimes even partnering up and expanding their businesses. They are able to connect with friends and agencies, and great business has grown from that. He has followed the Law of Action every year while creating his conferences and has watched them grow and thrive. He says:

"As I look back, this is what I know. You definitely have to set a goal and achieve it by creating actionable steps. Then you have to hustle. What's crazy about it is, anything can be done in three years. You just start writing down specific goals, no matter how pie-in-the-sky. Then you reverse engineer the steps down to smaller and smaller goals that can span a three-year period.

It all comes back down to your goal, your actionable steps, and your circle of influence. If that's not where it needs to be, reach out and partner up. There's something divine about it. Setting a good goal, having a solid action plan, and involving people who have a vested interest in the process allows you to create things that change the world."

When you can do what you love and get paid for it, you are a success. My four-year-old self knew I wanted to talk on TV. Now that's one thing I do, and I love it. I am so blessed that my passion supports my life. I'm well compensated for it, and it's a whole lot of fun. I love doing voiceovers. There's nothing better.

Life is so short and precious. If you are doing work that you hate just for the money, remember that money is great, but the most amazing thing is when you can do what you love *and* get well-rewarded financially.

People talk about "living the dream," but it's become this sarcastic thing. When I say I'm living the dream, I mean that I'm living the life I'd always dreamed of.

When you use the Law of Action to Decide, Plan and Act, you get to choose "what you wanna be when you grow up." It's your life, and growing up means you are finally being true to yourself.

If you're not where you want to be, take a leap of faith and go somewhere else. (Mind you, I'm not suggesting you quit your job without any regard to the consequences, financially or otherwise. Instead, use the Law of Action *now,* on the side of your current responsibilities if need be, to start taking steps in the right direction.)

That leads me into the story about my two dear friends who worked corporate jobs before we bought the hot rod shop. They were both very successful but were ready to take a leap of faith, so they invited me to join them in building one of the coolest, most badass shops in the country, Mods Hot Rods.

I love beautiful things, especially beautiful cars. Being a partner in Mods puts me in the position to be around incredible cars. They are works of art, which is something I can deeply appreciate.

My partners, Shawn and Nate, are passionate about cars. I love listening to them talk about their experiences and stories and hearing the excitement in their voice.

I asked Shawn what it was like to be actually "living the dream." Here's what he had to say...

SHAWN:

For as long as I can remember, I have been obsessed with cars. If it had tires and an engine, I was hooked. It started out with Hot Wheels. I had tons of them. I'd make little roads in the dirt all around our house and play with them for hours.

As I got older, I graduated to Stompers. I'm not sure if anyone else remembers Stompers, but they were little motorized cars with big rubber tires. They would take a single AA battery, and you could turn them on and watch them climb over any obstacle. Once again, I was back to building roads all throughout the yard to see how far I could push them. It wasn't long before I found ways to modify them, making them stronger, faster and bigger. And, of course, I had to find ways to put cooler paint jobs on them.

In my junior high years, I graduated to building model cars, which I enjoyed all through high school as well. (Looking back, maybe I shouldn't wonder as much why I didn't get many dates...) My passion for things with tires and engines continued to grow. I quickly realized that as much fun as it was to build models and play with toys, it would be even more fun to be in the middle of the action.

My first taste of motorized freedom came after my uncle dropped off a mini bike frame he had found abandoned in an alleyway. It needed a lot of work, but I was up for the challenge. I was fourteen at the time, and I did odd jobs and mowed lawns to save up money so I could purchase the parts to get the mini bike assembled again. After I got the parts, I realized I needed the skills to build as well.

My grandfather taught me how to rebuild an old lawn mower engine. I learned how to weld from my uncle and got the frame put back together again. Getting it to go was all I could think about. The first time I fired it up and rode it down the driveway, I was in heaven. This was also the first time I learned that 'whoa' was just as important as 'go,' but that's a story for another time. I had taken my maiden voyage, and it was better than I had ever dreamed. I had the ability to go anywhere my two little wheels could take me. Freedom was found, and my passion for vehicles continued to grow. After piecing together several more go-karts and mini bikes found in junkyards, alleyways and scrap yards, I finally turned sixteen.

Although there was always the family minivan and the old farm truck to drive, I had much bigger plans. I had inherited a 1951 Chevy truck from my father; it was the coolest thing I had ever seen. I'll interject here that I have always had a tendency to see things for what they could be and not what they currently are. As I looked at this old truck and saw what it would become, my sisters just saw a whole lot of work that wasn't worth doing and thought I had lost my mind. Despite the size of the task in front of me, I began the process of getting the truck back on the road. It was what I wanted to drive in high school, and all I could see were the amazing changes it would bring to my life. It took me several years to complete the project, but, with the help of my family, I restored my first classic vehicle by the end of my senior year of high school. I loved my truck, and I loved the process.

After high school, I allowed myself to be influenced by others. Instead of continuing to follow my passion, I followed expectations set on me. I began to be controlled by my life instead of keeping my hands on the steering wheel.

My decisions were based off the immediate need to survive, and my vision of the future became narrowed. I continued to work on cars here and there, started building another truck, and even purchased a motorcycle. I was working a job because it paid the bills, not because it was what I wanted to do. I viewed jobs in the auto industry the same way someone on a diet might stare longingly at doughnuts through a bakery window. I felt like the career I dreamed about and truly wanted was right there in front of me, but I couldn't touch it through the glass. I had created this illusion that having fun working on cars was a dream, and dreams were something to be enjoyed in your head as an escape while working your 'real' job in the 'real' world. It would be a long time before I realized that my thinking was wrong.

Although I would eventually break through the glass, first I pursued 'The American Dream.' I met a girl, got married, bought a house and had some kids.

Despite switching jobs, getting my bachelor's degree, and becoming very successful in corporate America, I continued to play with cars and fantasize about making a living that way. Any time the dream got too close, though, I would end up with my face smashed up against the glass and I would back off, discouraged.

I was content enough with my job in the software industry. It paid me well, and I was able to enjoy my dream on the weekends, tinkering on my own project cars from time to time and going to every car show I could squeeze into my busy schedule. Looking back, I even remember a time when I was walking through a car show with Rob as we joked, talked and dreamed about owning a hot rod shop someday. You know, 'someday,' the word you use when you don't think something will ever actually happen, but you're not going to say it out loud.

I didn't stop dreaming of cars. I spent every spare moment I had admiring rebuilt custom cars and seeing the possibilities of broken heaps being turned into works of art. I constantly followed my favorite builders and was always searching Craigslist and eBay for cars I wished I could buy.

Then my life changed.

At the time, I had no idea it was about to be turned upside down. After thirteen years of employment, the company I had been working for was sold. The owner was a great man, and I was really happy for him. The new owner, Steve, seemed like a good guy as well.

I looked forward to what I thought would be the chance to find new enjoyment in my day-to-day job. Unfortunately, not much changed, and after several months I realized I was still in the same trenches. I went back to dreaming about cars all the time.

Looking for an escape, I searched for a new corporate job, but things never worked out and it was getting frustrating. I still had a good job, but I wasn't really happy. It was a weird place to be. On one hand, I had it pretty good, working where I was treated well, with great people whom I enjoyed being around.

I was paid well, worked close to home, and even had pretty flexible hours. I had everything I had ever dreamed about when I was in college, so what was the problem? Why couldn't I just be happy? In those moments, I would always think about how cool it would be to just work on cars all day.

Then I would stuff those thoughts back down and get back to my 'real' life. I did not realize at the time what I was going through, but it all became clear one day when I was meeting with Steve. He told me the story of his own career path and how he came to the decision to follow his dream of buying a software company. Something clicked in my head.

Shortly after that conversation, I asked him about the elephant statue he kept in his office in a prominent place. He told me that it had been a gift and that it was the Hindu God, Ganesha, who would knock down obstacles in your path. I'm not Hindu, so I'm sure there is more to it than that, but I walked out of his office thinking about what he had said.

He had followed his dream. Then one day it hit me like a brick to my face. As I sat in my office pondering my life, I watched Steve walk by. I began to think how lucky he was to be able to live his dream and buy such a cool company. I asked myself what made him so special; why was he able to follow his dream? What made him different from me?

The answer I got back changed my life.

Nothing.

There was nothing special about him. He was just like me!

He might have grown up in a different family or taken a different career path prior to buying our company, but the truth was, he was no different than me. There was literally nothing special about him.

That thought bounced around in my head like crazy. Wait, how could that be? There had to be something special to be able to go after his dream! I continued to analyze it, but the answer to every question or scenario I could come up with was no different than the opportunities I had in my own life.

The only difference between us was what he was choosing to do. He CHOSE to live his dream instead of looking at it through the glass. The final thought came to me as simple as it could be: if HE could do it, then I could do it.

The glass wall I had created...shattered. With that one realization, my entire life changed.

I will never forget that moment. After thirteen years in the corporate world, it became so obvious, I felt stupid. It was like realizing all I needed to do to get to the doughnuts was walk through the front door instead of standing there drooling on the glass.

From that moment on, my mission became figuring out how to accomplish and live my dream. I had seen what was possible and could no longer sit idly by. Through a lot of research on the Internet and speaking to anyone who had any knowledge on the subject, I began to learn how and where businesses were bought and sold.

My first search on BizBuySell.com yielded several results for mechanic shops, including a hot rod shop that was for sale.

I stared at it in disbelief and then quickly sent an email to the broker selling the business. As much as I wanted that dream to come true, the size and cost of the business was more than I could bear alone. I continued to look at smaller shops. After three months of keeping this process to myself and my immediate family, I began to get brave and tell others of my plans. During this time, I started to let my friends in on my new reality and what I had discovered. Surprisingly, some thought I was crazy, whereas others who were already living their own dreams wondered why it had taken me so long.

Overall, it was good to be validated, and the support I received from friends and family was positive and encouraging. I was determined to walk this new path alone, to be the master of my own destiny, but a few of my friends had other plans.

To my pleasant surprise, I was joined by two of my friends: my current business partners, Nate and Rob. With their support, my dreams expanded further, and the hot rod shop I once thought out of my reach became possible. We met as a group many times, sometimes late at night, planning each step. The overall process in purchasing the shop wasn't all cupcakes and rainbows; it took a lot of work and determination. We all had to sacrifice a lot to make owning the shop a reality, but I knew that it was possible, and there was no turning back.

My entire life had changed, and something I had long dreamed about was now becoming my 'real' life. All because of the simple realization that I could actually live my dream by simply taking action.

Now, I get to work on cars, with Nate, every day. It's interesting how parallel our stories are.

Being in business with one good friend is incredible; I have the pleasure of being in business with two of my dear friends. My twenty-eight-year-old friend, Nate, has been on this ride with Shawn and me. I asked Nate to share with me his version of his process of taking action to live his dream.

NATE:

In 2015, I was finding myself in a rut at work, at home, in friendships, and with myself. I struggled to find meaning in any of these relationships and knew that if I did not make a plan to better myself, I would forever be diving into the unknown. I live the words in Provehito en Altum. We all have our own wilderness to traverse, but a roadmap makes it easier to get through it.

I knew that in order for me to get out of this rut, I needed to understand what the root cause of my unhappiness was. I sat down one night and wrote everything that was making me unhappy on a white piece of paper. It all led to where I was working, but it didn't make sense. I had a great career with a new startup tech company based out of New York. Benefits included unlimited vacation, free healthcare for my whole family, free lunch every day, stock options, great people to work with, and lots of opportunities for growth. However, I have never enjoyed working for someone else. This was my greatest issue.

A little background about my entrepreneurial endeavors: I started a lawn mowing company when I was twelve years old and babysat on the weekends to save money for my first pickup truck. I also started a pool company to help pay for college. I have always enjoyed working for myself, and I have been great at running small businesses. I had to make a decision in regard to my unhappiness: stay at a cush job or step out and work for myself again.

During this time, I had a lot of support from my wife, family, and friends to step out on my own. I had a friend, Shawn, who was as crazy as I was to step out with me so we could work for ourselves. Shawn was very successful working for a tech company as well but knew that it was time for a shift in his career. Shawn and I knew that we wanted to do something in the automotive world. We made a plan to visit every tire store, mechanic shop, engine rebuilding, and lube service that was for sale in the Phoenix area, and we did.

After nine months of searching, we narrowed it down to a mechanic shop in Gilbert and an engine-rebuilding facility in Phoenix. However, something did not feel right about these places. So we went back online to see if there was something we were missing, and we found the hot rod shop that was for sale in Fountain Hills, AZ. We contacted the broker and scheduled a time to check out the shop.

We checked out Mods for Rods and fell in love with it. We saw great opportunity and the ability to do something we both loved. We pursued Mods hard and jumped through every hoop that was thrown at us. We spent three months finding every available dollar we had to come up with the down payment, which included adding an additional business partner: Rob. After 318 emails, a six-figure start-up fund, countless hours on the phone, hundreds of meetings with the broker, and thousands of text messages, we owned Mods Hot Rods.

We were constantly recreating a new plan to fit the needs of the broker, the bank, and the previous owners. We were scrappy, smart, and felt a sense of great pride when we came out on the other side owning a hot rod shop. There were days where we felt that the bank was not going to approve our loan, or something would upset the previous owners and they were going to back out of the deal. As cliché as it sounds, this was the greatest roller coaster of emotions I have ever experienced. I was twenty-eight years old and felt I had to prove myself to every new contact we would meet.

There were days where it felt like our actions were going to destroy the deal between us and the previous owners of Mods. Anxiety would settle in at night when we laid our heads down to sleep, making it extremely difficult to function. Marcus Aurelius said it best, "When you arise in the morning think of what a privilege it is to be alive, to think, to enjoy, to love..." (Side note, I highly recommend *Meditations* by Marcus Aurelius, the biography of Marcus and his insight to stoic philosophy.) I try my best to live every day by this sound wisdom, and know that every day is a privilege to act on our wants and needs. If you find yourself trying to take action, know that this has been a common struggle for mankind. Surround yourself with great people, and take action. Dive into the unknown.

We all have different dreams; only you can decide if your dream is right for you. Don't let others kill your dream. Imagine what's possible. Decide to do, plan how to do it, and then act. If you need to ask for advice, keep in mind the old saying: "Don't ask for advice from broke friends." What that means is consult with people who have had success and failures and success again; don't ask your broke-ass friends!

 ## Take a moment, and pause.

Things to think about:

- Are you happy in your work, or giving your energy to someone else's dreams?

- What do you love doing that comes easily for you? What would it be like to get paid to do it?

- What would you have to do to make that decision, and use The Law of Action to love your job so much you never feel like it's work?

Chapter 7

TAKING INSPIRED ACTION

"The path to success is to take massive, determined action."

-TONY ROBBINS

"A life lived of choice is a life of conscious action. A life lived of chance is a life of unconscious creation."

-NEALE DONALD WALSCH

THINKING ABOUT EVERYTHING IN THIS BOOK SO FAR, there have been a few examples of people who didn't act. But what would happen if the Plan part was left out; what might that create? I interviewed a good friend of mine, Christa, who experienced exactly that.

She took action without any planning. She got results, but it was not ideal. She shares below about her business life and a very personal story.

ROB:

So, what are you all about, Christa?

CHRISTA:

I'm a photographer specializing in women's portrait photography, as well as a speaker, educator and author of *The Art of Boudoir Photography: How to Create Stunning Photographs of Women*. I have a successful portrait business, and I've created a few different courses for fellow photographers on how to shoot beautiful photographs. I've taught internationally and spoken at a lot of photography trade shows around the world. I'm currently living in New York City with my husband and my awesome nine-year-old bonus daughter, and we're expecting a new member to the family this summer.

ROB:

Wow, you've accomplished a lot! But I know you had an experience where you missed a critical step of the Law of Action: the Plan phase. What happened; can you tell that story?

CHRISTA:

Yes. If you know me at all, you know I'm persistent. If I make a decision or a goal, I'm going to get there. It's unusual for me to *not* get there in some way. In 2010, I started with a business coach, and my goal was to make a million dollars. I made the decision, but I didn't really have a plan. I just thought a big commitment and desire was enough, and I didn't have a smart plan or any plan, really, other than to make more money than I was currently making.

That was silly, and of course I didn't make a million dollars that year because I had no plan, and therefore the action I took was not targeted in any way. It was just random action, which is better than no action, but you've got to marry it to something. You must have a step-by-step idea of what you're doing.

ROB:

So that one decision to not follow the Law of Action completely, by you just deciding and taking action and not planning or following the steps, actually stopped you from making a million dollars.

CHRISTA:

Yes, absolutely. One hundred percent. You cannot skip a step of Decide, Plan, Act. I skipped the Plan. I was so gung ho, and I just thought, "You just do more of what you're doing." That was really not a good plan. Sometimes you need experts to model if you're unsure what your plan should be. That's where a lot of people stop—they're unsure what to do next. Sometimes I know what I want next, but I don't know how to get there. I need to find someone to help me figure out how to close the gap, identify the step-by-step, and keep focused so as not to get overwhelmed by it. Also, take it one step at a time. I didn't know where to start, so I never had a plan. That really was ineffective.

ROB:

Okay. So where are you now that you decided, then you came up with a plan, then you acted. Did you get your million dollars?

CHRISTA:

Yes, I totally did! I have a practical, multi-step, insanely detailed plan, and in fact, I learned so much from that lesson that this is what I do for other people now. My new program is to give photographers a step-by-step plan and the mentoring to show them how to get from where they are to making six figures in their portrait photography business.

ROB:

Now what have you done where you decided, you planned, and overcame whatever challenges came up to actually put it into action?

CHRISTA:

Well, the biggest example is from my personal life, and that's when I was trying to conceive with my husband. The ultimate goal was to have a baby. I can't even pinpoint when there was a decision, because this is something I knew I always wanted. It was just a matter of meeting the right person, so the decision I guess comes when you will do anything in your power to make it happen. It was a real, 100 percent commitment. I was certain I would do this, that no matter what, I would make it happen.

There was a plan. We started with what most people would consider a normal approach to trying to conceive. We tried naturally for six months, and when that didn't work we went to the doctor and got checked out. We did every textbook thing, but we also developed a massive plan of action. You might have a plan, but you need to adapt it to your circumstances and the feedback you're getting. Regardless of any plan we previously created, I adapted and took massive, massive action.

I did everything within my power that I could. When you are dealing with fertility, so much of your world is not within your control, so I took massive action on training my mindset, because it is rough. Anyone who's been through it knows it is devastating. In fact, women who are trying to conceive have tested at the same stress levels as someone going through a terminal disease. That's how hard it is, and it is financially and emotionally devastating. My husband and I tried to conceive for five years, and we had so many ups and downs and setbacks and obstacles. We had different doctors telling us different things, so we didn't have a plan laid out for us by any one person. We had to make decisions and then try this and try that and then try this other thing.

We had some success and then we'd have a loss, and then we'd run out of money. We weren't able to afford twenty grand for IVF in Manhattan, so we had to come up with an alternate plan. We went to Greece where it's 3,000 euros, so we had to constantly adapt and gather more information and then go with our gut, ultimately.

There will be a lot of times when you'll hear advice about what you should do next, and most of it is give up, quit, or find something else. I believe you just have to stay committed to your vision. Not your plan, because your plan is going to change, but as long as you stay committed to your decision and you know in your gut, heart, and soul that this is what is meant for you, then you'll be successful.

It might not look like your original vision of what success is. Ideally, we would've gotten pregnant naturally in the first six months, and my stepdaughter would have a sibling more her age. It looks a little different, but it's still success because we're pregnant and expecting in July now. I can fill a whole book with everything we had to take action on and the million obstacles we had to find a way around.

ROB:

That's an incredible story! How did you push forward and stick with it?

CHRISTA:

Well, there was a lot of fear to overcome. I don't like taking even aspirin, and I had to take major drugs. I had to have a few different surgeries. My husband got mentally exhausted after four years and just wanted to stop. I was determined, though. I did a few different things. I got support. Fertility struggles are a very lonely business, and you need more support than just you and your partner. If you're on your own, it's even harder. I found a few different support networks for me. There are amazing people out there who can support you and listen and validate what you're going through. They also have resources and ideas that are helpful. I've found women to be the most helpful, nurturing, supportive community, especially women who are trying to conceive or have been there. I had a fertility coach who's a dear friend of mine, and I also had a therapist who would talk with me on a weekly basis and kept me sane.

I also had my mom, my best girlfriends, and my husband, and sometimes I was just at the end of my rope and just needed to cry it out or scream into a pillow. I just let myself have emotions, but here's the trick: I didn't let myself sit in them, because that erodes your commitment to your decision and takes you out of action and into an indecisive, inactive, inert state. The emotion has to move. Go through it. I was real, and I let myself have those emotions—which were all over the place for five years—but I tried not to let myself sit in them. I also tried to remember what I'm grateful for. After four and a half years of feeling like there was zero progress, I actually assessed everything we had accomplished, all the action we had taken, all the things we learned that didn't work, and I stayed with that one decision to not to give up and keep committed to our dream.

Never give up. Follow inspired action. Stick to the plan, and listen to your intuition.

Was using the Law of Action to become part owner of a hot rod shop an inspired action? You better believe it was.

It was the little voice that made me do it!

Do you listen to that voice? It's called your intuition.

It's the little voice that wakes you up and nudges you when you aren't sure about something.

Your intuition is basically a more expanded version of yourself. It has less limitations than the self-talk than can be present in our chattery minds.

Our minds are powerful, and we can use them to create or destroy our lives without even being aware we are doing it! The mind can create fear, which prevents us from moving forward in our lives. The intuition is the voice that always wants you on your best path.

That reminds me of an amazing dear friend named Ember who lives in Maui...

Ember, is an experiential transformation coach who uses Rapid Transformational Therapy™, Neuromovement™, and the Wim Hof

Method™ to bring about massive changes for people. I'm totally stoked by what she does and asked her if I could talk about her in my book, because the Law of Action is definitely about facing fear and making massive changes.

There are so many ways to face fears. How does getting into a bathtub of ice water sound?

Ember explained the Wim Hof Method™ to me as a process using the three pillars of breath, mindset, and cold exposure together with specific techniques so a person can learn to use their breath to influence different systems of their body. I couldn't understand why anyone would want to do that, so I asked her to elaborate. Ember talked about how many people are terrified of the cold, but this method allows entering a very cold state to be safe because it's a controlled therapeutic environment. There is a breathing meditation first, then the person experiences exposure through cold showers and, finally, full-on immersion into ice baths. A big benefit to this method is the part where you face your fear, by overcoming the mind's resistance to cold. That makes sense to me. This "controlled stress" practice is a workout for your cardiovascular, nervous, and respiratory systems, all guided by the mind. You learn to control your autonomic responses and "reset" your nervous system for resilience and adaptability. By tapping into the power of oxygen and cold exposure, one can unlock potential benefits to strengthen immune function, increase energy and metabolism, decrease inflammation, relieve pain, reduce stress, overcome fears, boost athletic performance, recover faster, sleep better and improve mood!

She even said that people have learned to transcend chronic pain with the breath and cold therapy. I'm not a doctor—and have never played one on TV—so I'm not giving medical advice here, but that makes sense to me. Ember called the ice bath the "fountain of youth." I wanted to understand even more when I heard that!

If this sounds interesting to you, you can try the exercise below. (I know I am going to.) Please listen to your body, mind, and healthcare professionals before trying any method like this. If you are pregnant or have epilepsy, DO NOT do this method. Make sure you are ready, and in your planning, consider getting the help of a trained Wim Hof Method™ professional or find a workshop near you at WimHofMethod.com.

Using the Law of Action to Take a Cold Shower (and Like it)

- **Decide** that you are going to turn the water all the way to cold after your regular shower. You will stay in it for fifteen to sixty seconds and commit to listening to your body's responses. You are open to experiencing health benefits from this practice. You will plan and prepare before acting.

- **Plan:** You are going to mentally prepare for this because it is new. You will listen to your intuition and ask for help before attempting anything that you are afraid of. You can ask for the help and support you need. You will listen to your body's responses and act according to what you need.

- **Act:** You will turn the water to cold for fifteen to sixty seconds, increasing the time each day until you reach a place where it actually feels good. Your cardiovascular system will love having the stimulus of going to the extreme of the vasodilation and the vasoconstriction.

ıber also gave me an empowering guided meditation to share. It can be used before trying this method, or any time you need to become centered again. You might want to read it slowly into your phone's voice recorder and play it back while resting.

Feel the surface you are resting on fully supporting you, and let go of all tension. Notice HOW you are lying. What areas of your body make contact with the surface supporting you? Breathe in to the abdomen...and...let it out gently. Breathe in fully, deeply again, then let it all go. Now breathe fully in and HOLD the breath. Tense the muscles of your whole body, squeeze them all tight, and HOLD the tension...and then...completely relax everything. Once more, inhale fully and tighten everything... HOLDING...HOLDING...HOLDING... And let...it...ALL...GO. Starting at your toes and moving upward, scan your body for any tightness that might remain. With your next inhale, direct your breath, with your intention, into that area of constriction and see it dissolving. Any residual tension flows out, all the way out, on the exhale.

With your new understanding, you are no longer bound by indecision and inaction. You are forever liberated from self-doubt because you know that each moment presents an opportunity to choose anew. You fully appreciate that massive results are achieved from wise planning and consistent, progressive actions.

Imagine yourself standing, poised to act with conviction and certainty. Feel the exhilaration and joy of anticipation. What decisions will you take action on next? See yourself in each scene moving through, and carrying out, your next important actions...

You know what to do, and you do it in the most perfect timing.

You know that when you move into action, the universe moves to meet you, opening doors on your behalf. Breathe IN... You ARE the inspiration...ready to move forward, clear, confident, and fully alive in YOUR EMPOWERED ACTION.

Every day, you will see the results of your actions building to create the world you desire. Your vision for that world is so compelling that it infuses itself into everything you do, energizing your actions. You feel incredibly fulfilled by the certainty that you are creating a brighter future for all. This is a source of boundless energy and unlimited motivation. Old patterns of self-doubt and fear no longer influence you. The past is NOT you. It is behind you, and it cannot ever affect you again. You know there IS NOTHING to fear because choice and action create the possibilities of tomorrow. There is nothing to doubt because each action brings greater clarity toward the future you desire. You know with unshakable conviction that YOU CANNOT FAIL. Failure DOES NOT exist. You know that unexpected results offer valuable information for realigning and refining future actions.

You are a confident and enthusiastic action taker. You feel such gratitude for the awakening of this great power within you. As you inhale each deep cleansing breath, you know with unwavering certainty that you now exemplify inspired action.

Take this power with you into your next action. It is time to come back now.

Feel the place where your body meets the surface you are resting on. Begin to make slight movement, wiggle your toes or gently stretch. Continue to breathe, and, before opening your eyes, move them from side to side and up and down. When you feel you are ready, open your eyes and continue your day with mindfulness and clarity.

Ember isn't just talking the talk; she has overcome a lot and has an amazing ability I admire: she is a free-diver. That basically means she can dive underwater without a tank and hold her breath for five minutes. It takes an incredible amount of self-discipline and training to be able to do that. She overcame the fear in a controlled and safe environment because she really wanted to do it. Now, she has awareness of and control over her fear response, her breath, and her mind. It's incredible. When I was talking about taking a cold shower, I mentioned listening to your body's messages and intuition. Those messages are there to guide and support you in taking the action that's best for you. Intuition will send an alert right through your body if there is danger, so don't ignore it! Even though Ember has trained to free-dive, it can still be dangerous. Her intuition helps keep her safe by telling her body there is danger, and her ability to respond without panicking is critical to her safety.

That's really a high level of connection to herself. I admire her ability to trust herself and the process so deeply. It's beautiful.

Your intuition is connected to feelings. If you aren't sure about something, stop what you're doing and check in with it. This may seem insignificant, but it can have huge implications. The Law of Action applies here as well; taking a moment to stop and tune in can prevent you from taking action on things that won't help you.

Using the Law of Action to Tune into Your Intuition

- **Decide:** When there is confusion, decide to slow down and check in. Instead of getting into drama and conversation, or letting your mind overanalyze the situation, simply feel into it.

- **Plan:** Consider the topic at hand and the desired result. Figure out the question you need to ask yourself to discover YOUR truth.

- **Act:** Take three deep breaths and ask the question, then be still, wait, and listen. What do you feel? The right choice will feel good. Yeah, it's that simple.

Once you make a habit of slowing down and checking in, your intuition will help guide you to what is right. Even if you have ADD or a busy mind, you can wrangle that squirrel. I am an idea factory; I think of things all the time. It can be distracting, but when I focus on what I'm good at and what feels good, everything flows in a wonderful way.

It's kind of like when salmon swim upstream to spawn.

They have a purpose to swim upstream at that time, but the rest of the time, they don't fight the flow.

Because, let's face it; swimming upstream is difficult! People do it all the time until they figure out that it's easier to go with the flow. Live your life as a salmon going downstream, not upstream. Sit back, relax, and enjoy the ride.

You'll need to paddle and take action to keep your raft going the right direction, but mainly you get to enjoy the ride.

Think of your intuition as your tour guide. It wants you to see all the good stuff. It's the little voice that wakes you up and shows you the best things in life if you listen.

Make friends with it and listen to it, and it will guide you.

Once you get good at hearing your intuition, all you have to do is pause and contemplate, "What's the right thing to do?"

Then listen, and you'll know the right path. If you're following your life purpose and taking action, you will get where you want to go.

Taming the Squirrel Brain

Our amazing minds can create so many thoughts and ideas at once that we can get stuck. We don't know which idea to follow or what action to take. When I learned about meditation, I figured out that it isn't just for yogis who sit on top of mountains; it's a useful tool to tame the busy squirrel brain. It's especially useful for someone with ADD.

Imagine standing on the bank of a whitewater rapids sort of river. One that surges fast and furious, with so much going by that it's hard to see any of it. Maybe a branch rushes by, carried by the water, but it's moving too fast to even see it.

My mind is like that river (can you relate?). The water is all of the thoughts, and the branch is a great idea. I can't get much accomplished when my mind is running that fast. The branch goes by, and I miss it.

Meditation helps me slow the river down.

The water still has the same volume, but it's smoother, and when a branch floats by, I can see it clearly and even grab it if I want to.

Meditation is a mystery to a lot of people. They wonder, *How do you meditate? What is it all about?*

There are many methods and ideas, but I suggest you start with a guided meditation. I'll share a sample here in a minute. Guided meditations put the thoughts in your mind for you so you have something to focus on. If you are new to meditation, you will probably find that helpful.

Once you get the hang of it, you can try silent meditation, or maybe music meditation, or prayers or mantras. There are plenty of varieties to suit what you need. The following meditation sample gives you an idea of what it's like. You can find countless meditations on YouTube as well. (If you like these meditations, I've produced the meditations in this book and a few other surprises as a gift to you, available for no-cost download at TheLawofAction.com/bonus.)

Obviously, it's nice to close your eyes to meditate, so you might consider recording yourself reading this (using the audio recorder available on most phones) and then listening to it. (If you're driving in your car and listening to the audio book version of this book, don't close your eyes! Come on, we're all responsible adults. Find a quiet, safe space to do this meditation. I may have added this disclaimer due to the story of the lady who scalded herself with hot coffee at the drive-through. But I digress...)

Meditation Sample

Sit down in a quiet place. Make sure your whole body is as relaxed and comfortable as possible. Breathe in and out without trying to change the way you are breathing. Just notice your breath.

Are you breathing shallow or deep?

Does bringing awareness to your breath make you change the way you breathe? Continue to breathe in and breathe out. Just relax. Be in the moment.

This moment is yours, all for you. If any stressful thoughts come up, notice them and let them float away. There is plenty of time to respond to them later. Right now, it's just time to breathe.

You have nothing else to do, nowhere else to go. It's time to be still. You are recharging and becoming clear so when you are taking action again, you can do so powerfully. Keep breathing, in and out. Notice your body and how it feels as you breathe. If there is discomfort, put your awareness on it, and notice where it is. You can shift your position to relieve discomfort, or simply notice it so you can take care of it later.

Notice the temperature of the room, and feel the air contacting your skin and the difference in temperature of your bare skin compared to skin that is covered by clothing. Are you comfortable? Just notice it.

What thoughts and voices are present in your mind? Can you let them all float by? Let all that squirrel chatter go. Turn down the volume so they are a quiet whisper. This is your time.

Now, take a big, deep breath in and hold it for a moment before releasing it. After you have exhaled completely, hold your breath for a moment and notice what that feels like.

Take several deep breaths now. In and out, holding your breath slightly between inhaling and exhaling.

Start to reconnect to your body. Wiggle your fingers or toes and begin to move ever so slightly. Bring your awareness to your eyes and how they feel behind your closed eyelids. Without opening your eyes yet, look left and right, up and down. Feel the tiny muscles that move your eyes all day.

Now gently open your eyes.

After a meditation, return to mindfulness. Before you get up and go about your day, bring more and more awareness to every moment.

If you're like me, and you have difficulty focusing because your mind races a million miles a minute, mindfulness is something that can truly help.

Mindfulness is simply being present in the moment. The very moment of now.

Consider this.

As you go through your life, do you pay any attention to picking up a glass of water and drinking it?

Do you pay any attention when putting food in your mouth? To the chewing, or the taste and texture of the food?

Do you pay attention when brushing your teeth to the feel of the bristles on your gums? Do you pay attention to the wind blowing outside? How about a fan or air conditioner blowing on your body?

Our world is so overstimulating that it can be easier to just shut out all of our senses. Many people don't feel much at all as they go through their day. It's a choice.

Using the Law of Action to Practice Mindfulness

- **Decide** to drink a glass of water. Pause for a moment, and imagine the whole process: what the glass looks like, how the water feels as you swallow it. Experience the refreshment.

- **Plan** every little step of drinking a glass of water. I am going to get up, walk to the kitchen, open the cabinet, get out a glass, walk to the water dispenser, bring the glass to the spout, open the spout, fill the glass, close the spout, lift the glass to my lips, open my mouth, pour the water in, swallow it, then lower the glass.

- **Take action** on this just as mindfully as you have spent time planning it. Be aware of each step as you go through it. Simply noticing this simple thing we do every day and finally paying attention to it has just brought you into the present moment.

You can use this for everything, to help connect to your senses.

When brushing your teeth, feel the bristles on your gums. Listen to the sound of the toothbrush going over your teeth. Taste the toothpaste. Use your tongue to notice the smoothness of your teeth after you are done.

All of this talk of mindfulness brings us back to taking inspired action. Slow down and be clear on what you are experiencing in each moment so you can check in and know your next move.

Decide, Plan, Act.

You ever have an amazing idea floating in your head and then see that someone else has created it?

Most of us have seen someone else's million-dollar idea that's come to life and said, "I should have done that."

Maybe you imagined that exact thing but never took action because you got stuck in planning.

If you don't take action, someone else will.

I believe that everybody has the same opportunity as everyone else.

I believe that ideas are just floating around for anyone to grab and bring into reality.

A lot of us will grasp onto an idea and decide that we're going to take action, and then we plan and we plan...and we plan...

But we don't act. We're not obeying the Law of Action, because the Act phase never gets done.

Think of the Pet Rock. Gary Dahl took a rock, put it in a box, called it a "pet rock" and became a multimillionaire.

It's such a simple idea. It is a ridiculously simple idea!

But what did he do? He decided. He planned. He acted.

There are lots of ideas out there. Bringing one into reality depends on you following through with the Law of Action.

Decide, Plan, Act.

The Value of Stories

Your story needs to be told. Your life experiences are worth sharing. Everything you have gone through has brought you to this moment, and there are many people going through that exact thing, so telling your story and how you got through it can help many people.

People love to hear stories. They connect us to experiences and adventures. They entertain and inspire us. We all hear stories in different ways.

Sometimes we interpret them differently than others, but we always get what we need for our life.

Do you remember Aesop's Fables?

They're little stories with a moral, or message, at the end. Most of them make sense, but one story in particular has always irritated me.

"The Tortoise and the Hare."

If you're not familiar with "The Tortoise and the Hare," it's a story about a hare, which is a large rabbit, and a big tortoise who compete in a race.

The hare has lots of energy and athletic ability, and he is a mover and a shaker who takes massive action. He's very confident about how fast he is.

Then there's a tortoise. He's big, clunky, and slow.

They're having a race, because the tortoise was told by the hare that he was not going to be able to beat the hare. There was no way he could ever beat the hare. He moves slow and steady, and the hare moves fast and furious.

That hare is a massive, immediate action taker.

I'm sure you know which character I relate to. Hint: my nickname is Thumper. For all you millennials out there, Thumper is from the classic animated Disney film, *Bambi*. (Spoiler alert: Bambi's mom dies.)

So, the tortoise and the hare line up at the starting line. The race starts.

The hare takes off at breakneck speed, while the tortoise plods along.

It doesn't take long before the hare realizes that he's way ahead, and he stops and talks to these really cute bunny girls. He plays tennis, he plays ping pong. He dances, he sings. He does all kinds of things. And he keeps seeing he's way ahead of the tortoise, so he takes a nap.

Now he's asleep, and the tortoise, who's just been plodding along the whole time, passes the hare. As he is just about to cross the finish line, all of the forest animals start cheering. The hare wakes up to the noise and sprints to the finish line, but he's too late. The tortoise has crossed the line and won the race.

So, the moral of the story is that slow and steady wins the race. Don't be a rabbit. Slow down, and take life slow and steady.

Well, I think that is not true in any shape or form.

I am the hare.

I take massive, immediate action, and I get things done.

I decide, I plan, I act.

Now, I also get distracted and go left and right, and—okay, being honest—I might stop to talk to cute bunny girls and sing and dance a bit.

I have a whole lot of fun in my life, but the thing is, I'm still moving forward.

What I've noticed about most successful people is they have taken the Law of Action into account.

They decide, they plan, they act. When they act, it's massive, immediate action.

When I was at the Ultimate Breakthrough event I mentioned earlier, I was sitting there, watching Ed Rush do a talk about how he feels that "The Tortoise and the Hare" story is just wrong. He then proceeded to say exactly what I just said. This told me two things. One, there are lots of ideas out there, and many other people have your exact same idea.

Two, it also told me that I was sitting at the right event! It's always great to learn from someone who is aligned with you.

My invitation to you is to not be a tortoise, because I believe—and many others have proven—that slow and steady does *not* win the race. Massive, immediate action wins the race.

You are worthy, and you can do this. Listen to your voice of intuition so you can take action on the right thing. Massive, immediate action.

Tell your story.

Bring your idea into the world.

Decide, Plan, Act.

CONCLUSION

EVERY MOMENT OF LIFE IS PRECIOUS, AND THE fact that you took time out of your life to read the words that I have put in this book is truly humbling. I am deeply honored to bring you what I believe is a life-saving concept: the Law of Action.

After many life experiences, it became crystal clear to me that the Law of Action was one of those ideas floating around that I had been using my whole life. It was time to share it with others. If this book helps just one person bring their idea into reality, it has all been worth it. My hope is that it inspires many, many people to take action. And that means *you.*

Since you've gotten this far in the book, you are an action taker. You're someone who decides, plans, and then acts. Congratulations. Most people don't finish books like you just did. I want you to have an extraordinary life, a life of joy and happiness, and one way to do that is by following the Law of Action: decide you want to do something, plan for it, and then go out and take action. I know that if you follow the Law of Action, doors will open in your life like you've never seen before. Opportunities that you never imagined in your wildest dreams will present themselves. When you break through your fear of success, your fear of failure, your fear of unworthiness, your fear of imperfection, your fear of rejection, or the big one: the imposter syndrome. Whatever fear you have, when you move from planning to action, your life will be better. And happier, too.

Sharing the Law of Action brings me immense joy, and I hope you've found as much happiness in reading it as I had in writing it.

ADDITIONAL GIFTS FOR YOU

I'VE COMPILED ALL OF THE "USING THE LAW of Action" examples from this book here for easy reference. The more you use Decide, Plan, Act, the easier it gets. The faster you repeat the process of the Law of Action, the more success you will experience.

Using the Law of Action to Get Dressed in the Morning

- **Decide** to get dressed for your day.

- **Plan** your clothing based on the day's activities, for example: *It's going to be a bit chilly, and I've got a client meeting, then lunch with a friend. The best thing to wear is, blah blah blah...*

- **Act** by getting dressed.

Using the Law of Action to Join a New Company

- **Decide** that you really like this product line and the results it gives people. It is helping people feel better. You feel good about the people who are inviting you, and you'd like to work with them. Thinking about this brings you joy. You are excited!

- **Plan** to do some research and check your resources to make sure you have the time and money to spend on this opportunity. Go in prepared to act and create a business.

- **Act** by becoming part of the team and devoting time to sharing and promoting this company and its products.

Using the Law of Action to Create Beneficial Lists

- **Decide** what the list is for; limit it to a single project or put a short time frame on it with a specific deadline (preferably in the near future).

- **Plan** the result before making the list. Think about the desired outcome, and imagine it is complete. Imagine the steps to get there.

- **Act** by writing the topic at the top of the list, then write steps SPECIFIC to the plan in a logical order. Look at your list, knowing the end result, and feel the joy of completing it, then take action and finish it!

Using the Law of Action to Reverse Engineer a Sandwich

- **Decide:** Close your eyes and imagine the finished sandwich in your hands. It's been neatly cut in half, so you can see all of the layers in it. What sort of bread do you use? Is it toasted? What's inside the sandwich? What condiments are on it?

- **Plan:** Now that you know what the sandwich looks like, get out the ingredients you need for your sandwich. If you are missing something, find a substitute, and maybe add it to a grocery list (which is a great use for a list, by the way).

- **Act:** Build your sandwich. The bread is the outer layer, right? The mayo (or peanut butter, mustard, etc.) get spread with a spoon or knife on the inside of the bread. These things seem so simple, we do them all the time without thinking. Next comes the lettuce, roast beef, ham, salami, provolone cheese, pickles, tomato, pesto, olives, feta cheese...whatever your sandwich needs, put it in the right order.

Using the Law of Action for Failures

- **Decide** that you are okay, because failure is part of success. Forgive yourself! Maybe step away for a bit, and let the emotion subside so you can get clear again.

- **Plan** to understand the failure's purpose and open yourself to be humble enough to get it. At the same time, decide not to make the same mistake again.

- **Act** by adjusting and retrying OR abandoning the thing you failed at and trying something new. In either case, go back to Decide.

Using the Law of Action for Personal Fitness and Health

- **Decide** that you are ready to feel great, fit, and healthy. Imagine looking in the mirror and seeing a strong, lean version of yourself.

- **Plan** to allow time to devote to your health and to connect with the right coach for you.

- **Act** by hiring a coach/trainer, showing up, and working out at home as well.

Using the Law of Action for Getting Your Dream Job

- **Decide** you are ready to receive the job offer of your dreams. Imagine what it feels like to have it. Really FEEL that excitement and know it's time to move into that job.

- **Plan** to accept that job by asking yourself, "What tangible things need to happen?" Listen to your inner guidance, thoughts and feelings. Take mental notes, then turn those into physical notes you can review. Be unrealistic and ambitious! You are about to have your dream job!

- **Act.** This may mean applying for a specific job or sending an amazing résumé to places you want to work for. Maybe it means making phone calls or putting word out to friends or social contacts. Do it.

Using the Law of Action for Finding Your Joy

- **Decide** you deserve to have fun and joy in your life. Feel that laughter and easy smile that you had when you were a kid. Kids are great at playing! Think about what simple things you enjoy now.

- **Plan** to spend one minute feeling joy every day, then increase it to five minutes, then an hour, then...three hours! You might have to actually SCHEDULE time to play until you get good at it. Put it on your calendar and devote time to it. Exercising your laughter muscles is just as important as working out, so give it that much priority.

- **Act** on creating your joy! Keep a humorous book by the toilet. Make a YouTube playlist of videos that make you smile, and watch one every day. Spend time with your kids or pets.

Using the Law of Action to Get Motivated

- **Decide:** Finding motivation means admitting that you aren't motivated yet, and you are ready to change that. It's really about personal responsibility. Your life is where it is as a result of every action you have taken, or not taken. Don't beat yourself up over this, just notice where you are and start from there. If you are deciding to "get motivated," you'll have to figure out why you haven't been before and change that behavior. Before you go to the planning step, be sure this decision is something you are ready for.

- **Plan:** Accountability will help turn self-motivation into a new habit. Find a partner who is also ready to be more motivated into taking action toward their goals and check in daily. The tide will rise, and all ships rise with it. Find people who are more motivated than you, and rise with them. Find simple things you know you should do but don't, like flossing your teeth and making your bed, and think about *why* you do or should do those things. For instance, flossing keeps your teeth healthier and less prone to cavities and other painful, expensive setbacks. When you know your why, motivation comes much easier.

- **Act:** Set yourself up for success by starting simple. As easy as it is to make your bed, do you do it? This is a great way to begin working with a partner and check in with each other without getting overwhelmed. Once this becomes a habit, add another action to do every day. Maybe...working out, meditating, journaling, doing the dishes or even making the bed?

Using the Law of Action to Get Help (Rob's Version)

- **Decide:** I decided I needed to restore my peace, and I knew I had no idea how. All I knew was that it was time, and it had to happen. I imagined living in my home with it feeling like a hotel. I wanted a place for everything and everything in its place. I saw it and felt it in my mind.

- **Plan:** I sent a message to the universe asking to be guided in getting this result. I had no idea what it meant; I only knew I couldn't do it alone. My "Plan" was to surrender and allow the right help to show up.

- **Act:** Within the next week, I met someone who would change my life. I didn't know what would happen, but I KNEW that she was the one I had asked for. I acted. I asked her, and I hired her! My action resulted in massive changes in my life.

Using the Law of Action to Meet Someone New (also Rob's Version!)

- **Decide:** I am interested in getting to know that person. I am attracted to them on some level and curious about them. I am going to initiate a connection.

- **Plan:** I will walk across the room and say hello. I will express my interest in getting to know them. I know that I may get rejected, but I am okay with it as long as I try.

- **Act:** I'm taking a deep breath to center my energy, then walking over and saying hello. I have no expectation of a result.

Using the Law of Action to Attract Money

- **Decide:** Feel the emotion of being wealthy and abundant. Imagine never hesitating to buy what you want, knowing your relationship with money is healthy and solid. Imagine opening your bank account and seeing a balance that's ten times what you are used to. Imagine opening your wallet and seeing several hundred-dollar bills in it.

- **Plan:** Choose a method to change your relationship with money. The *Magic Money* series by Holly Alexander or Ed Rush's *The 21-Day Miracle* are two amazingly powerful ways to get results. Commit to devoting time to actually DO THE WORK. Put it in your planner or calendar. Set alarms. You are reprogramming your mind, so plan a way that will work for you. Set small, measurable goals.

- **Act:** Begin following the plan you have made! Regardless of the method you use, you have to take action and put time and effort into sticking to it. Focus. Reward yourself as you go.

Using the Law of Action to Take a Cold Shower (and Like it)

- **Decide** that you are going to turn the water all the way to cold after your regular shower. You will stay in it for fifteen to sixty seconds and commit to listening to your body's responses. You are open to experiencing health benefits from this practice. You will plan and prepare before acting.

- **Plan:** You are going to mentally prepare for this because it is new. You will listen to your intuition and ask for help before attempting anything that you are afraid of. You can ask for the help and support you need. You will listen to your body's responses and act according to what you need.

- **Act:** You will turn the water to cold for fifteen to sixty seconds, increasing the time each day until you reach a place where it actually feels good. Your cardiovascular system will love having the stimulus of going to the extreme of the vasodilation and the vasoconstriction.

Using the Law of Action to Tune into Your Intuition

- **Decide:** When there is confusion, decide to slow down and check in. Instead of getting into drama and conversation, or letting your mind over analyze the situation, simply feel into it.

- **Plan:** Consider the topic at hand and the desired result. Figure out the question you need to ask yourself to discover YOUR truth.

- **Act:** Take three deep breaths and ask the question, then be still, wait, and listen. What do you feel? The right choice will feel good. Yeah, it's that simple.

Using the Law of Action to Practice Mindfulness

- **Decide** to drink a glass of water. Pause for a moment and imagine the whole process: what the glass looks like, how the water feels as you swallow it. Experience the refreshment.

- **Plan** every little step of drinking a glass of water. I am going to get up, walk to the kitchen, open the cabinet, get out a glass, walk to the water dispenser, bring the glass to the spout, open the spout, fill the glass, close the spout, lift the glass to my lips, open my mouth, pour the water in, swallow it, then lower the glass.

- **Take action** on this just as mindfully as you have spent time planning it. Be aware of each step as you go through it. Simply noticing this simple thing we do every day and finally paying attention to has just brought you into the present moment.

Suggested Reading

I READ A LOT OF BOOKS, AND I truly believe in the power within them, especially personal development books. I'm a better person because I've learned from masters. Here are some of the books I've read and loved; maybe you will, too.

The Miracle Morning - Hal Elrod

You Must Write a Book - Honorée Corder

The 21 Day Miracle - Ed Rush

Think and Grow Rich, Grow Rich with Peace of Mind, and

The Master Key to Riches - Napoleon Hill

Way of the Peaceful Warrior - Dan Millman

The Four Agreements - Don Miguel Ruiz

Conversations with God - Neale Donald Walsch

The Power of Now - Eckhart Tolle

Power of Intention - or ANYTHING by Dr. Wayne Dyer

How to Stop Worrying and Start Living - by Dale Carnegie

Rich Dad, Poor Dad - Robert Kiyosaki

Awaken the Giant Within - Tony Robbins

Leading an Inspired Life - Jim Rohn

The Road Less Traveled - Dr. M. Scott Peck

4-Hour Work Week - Tim Ferriss

ACKNOWLEDGEMENTS

AS I'M WRITING THIS BOOK, I FEEL SO much gratitude for the amazing people I have surrounded myself with. I know when I choose to spend time with amazing people, I will be challenged to raise the bar on my own life. That has happened in ways I had never imagined.

You find out who your real friends are when you go through difficult times. Back in chapter one, Aidan's story, I mentioned there were a few people who showed up powerfully for us.

It's hard to know what to say or do when someone is going through that much trauma, and I'd like to acknowledge a few people who showed up and sat with us through one of the most terrifying experiences of our lives.

First, with deep gratitude, is Derral Eves. I talked about Derral in chapter six but would like to share a little more here. In everyday life, Derral is not only a successful entrepreneur but also a family man from southern Utah. He is married, with five amazing kids.

One thing I admire about Derral is his attitude about people. Considering that Derral is an accomplished business man with huge successes, he remains humble. He told me this story about how he believes nobody is better than anyone else:

We're all people in this existence, and just because some people have more money in the bank account or are smarter at some things than you, it's not that big of a deal. They are still people, they just have different issues and different problems, depending on the baggage that they carry. I have never felt inferior to anyone, and I can give you a personal story about that.

I was flying out of Las Vegas on a red-eye to New York, and I was hungry. There really wasn't anything open except for a pretzel place, so I ordered the last pretzel. It had pepperoni on it. This guy came up and said, "Dude, I want that pretzel. You're gonna give it to me."

I responded, "I'm not gonna give you the pretzel. I just bought it. I'm not gonna just hand it to you."

As he asked, "Do you know who I am?" I said, "Yes, I do," as his bodyguard, who was about six foot eight and 400 pounds, came up and said, "You're gonna give him that pretzel."

I denied him the pretzel again, and he said, "Some people..."

I ate the pretzel in front of him and said, "Mr. Well-Known Hollywood Director, it's okay. You've got a lot of money and you've got a lot of time, so you can wait for your own pretzel."

Derral doesn't let people intimidate him. I asked him about the challenges he faces, and how he handles them. His attitude about life is so encouraging and inspiring. He talks about taking action to get through being discouraged:

Is there ever discouragement? Absolutely. People can get discouraged at any time, the question is, for how long? It lasts for only as long as you allow it to. I truly believe it. You can lick your wounds and say, "Woe is me," and really have struggles, and just be in a slump, and get depressed, or you can go out and do something different.

So, this is what I found: if you begin to lose yourself and start thinking, "Oh, I can't do this," or, "I can't be this person," or, "I'm not good enough," the easiest way to reverse that is to go out and serve someone else. Do something good for someone and be a better you. Then you'll realize that there isn't anything that you can't do. You can literally change a person's day. You can really become someone greater than who you are today just by looking for that opportunity to serve our fellow man and serve God.

Derral did exactly that for my family; he showed up. He served us. We will never forget it.

I could go on for pages in gratitude for people who have shown up for me in my life. I always do my best to let people know how much they mean to me.

From the very beginning, my mom. Thank you for always being supportive of me, even when you didn't understand how I could be successful just by following my desire to "talk on TV."

My dad, who was always supportive and proud of me. Thank you for being the one who showed up and sat in the booth to watch me speak on the radio for the first time on that Christmas Day.

My sister, Anita. For being my bonus mom and always being there for me. (And you said I couldn't write a book...)

My brother-in-law, Ed; there's nobody like you. You're the best, always kind and positive and willing to listen to all of my crazy ideas.

To Dennis, the one stepdad who was my bonus dad.

To my brother, David; thank you for your service to this country in the Army and for your unwavering support of my ideas, except the time I considered following your path and being a meat cutter...thanks so much for talking me out of that.

To my sister, Celeste, thank you for being so tolerant and putting up with your little brother, with me always wanting to have the radio on and not the TV.

And to my oldest brother, Jim, thank you for letting me read your textbooks from your radio class. I learned a lot; another stepping stone to my pursuit of being on the radio. You did it; you became a radio DJ, which showed me that it was possible and that even as a young kid, I was on the right path.

To Tony, you're a longtime dear friend and you're the major catalyst that got me into radio. And then a catalyst again in the voiceover industry.

To Andrea, thank you! I never knew that going through the Flowganize process would change my life so dramatically. You did it; you brought out my inner superhero.

To my dear friend Kenzie, thank you for all you do to support me in my life, especially all the great care you give to Stella (for those who are wondering, Stella is my eight-pound Chihuahua).

To my dear friends Shawn and Nate, my amazing friends and amazing business partners (yes, I meant to say "amazing" twice; editor Tammi said no, but I said yes!).

Thank you to my dear friends Paula and Jenny; your friendship and positivity means the world to me.

To everyone along my path in the radio and voice acting world, thank you.

To the crew at Q-News, a major launch pad for many successful careers.

To all the amazing people in my life, I know I've told you how much you mean to me, and if you're not included in this section, it in no way means I don't love you. I do! This book was written in *thirty days*, so as you can imagine my brain is fried.

However, I would never forget to acknowledge YOU, the reader of this book.

Connect with People in this Book

Chapter 2—Brian Anderson: Media Mash, mediamash.com and Voice Drops, voicedrops.net

Chapter 2—Ryan Bader, Bellator Light Heavyweight Champion of the World: www.facebook.com/ryanbader

Chapter 2—Jason Kamens: Instagram - @jasonkamens

Chapter 3—Bruce Caulk, Hollywood Writer/Director: www.imdb.com/name/nm3280849/, @reelbruce

Chapter 3—Bobby Rich, www.B100.fm

Chapter 3—Alison Lea Sher: www.facebook.com/alison.l.sher

Chapter 3—TopGolf, Gilbert, AZ: www.topgolf.com/us/gilbert/

Chapter 3—Costa Vida: costavida.com

Chapter 4—Tracy Enos, LinkedIn Expert: www.linkedin.com/in/tracyenos

Chapter 4—Tina Williams, Natural Wellness Advisor:
www.linkedin.com/in/williamstina/

Chapter 4—Honorée Corder, Author, Coach, Speaker:
www.honoreecorder.com

Chapter 4—Hal Elrod, *The Miracle Morning*: halelrod.com

Chapter 5—Andrea King, Flowganize: flowganize.com

Chapter 5—Holly Alexander, *Magic Money:*
www.facebook.com/holly.alexander.1042

Chapter 6—Darrel Eves, YouTube Expert: derraleves.com

Chapter 6—Shawn Smith: modshotrods.com

Chapter 6—Nate Judd: modshotrods.com

Chapter 7—Ember Behrendt: stokedforlife.com

Chapter 7—Christa Meola, Photographer: christameola.com

ABOUT THE AUTHOR

ROB ACTIS is the author of the #1 bestselling book *The Law of Action*. A lifelong go-getter, action taker and serial entrepreneur, Rob used the Law of Action to achieve his lifelong dream of speaking on TV, radio, and, to become a successful audiobook narrator of over 25 titles available on Audible.com.

Look for popular audio book titles such as:

- *The Miracle Morning* book, and complete series by Hal Elrod and Honorée Corder

- *You Must Write a Book* - Honorée Corder

- *Write Like a Boss Series* - Honorée Corder and Ben Hale

- *Becoming Your Best* - Steve Shallenberger

- *Magic Money Series* - Holly Alexander

- Napoleon Hill classics *Grow Rich with Peace of Mind* and *The Master Key to Riches*

Rob is now on a mission to help others wake up to their raw potential and take the actions needed to create amazing lives. You can learn more at **www.RobActis.com**.

ONE LAST THING...

IF YOU ENJOYED THIS BOOK OR FOUND IT useful, I'd be very grateful if you'd post a short review on Amazon and share it with any friends who might find it helpful. Your support really does make a difference and I read all the reviews so I can get your feedback and make my books the best they can be.

> If you'd like to leave a review, all you need to do is click the review link on this book's page on Amazon here:
> **https://tinyurl.com/LawOfAction**

Thanks again for your support!

Made in the USA
San Bernardino, CA
11 June 2018